Praise for *Promises Unbroken: Exploring God's Covenant of Love from Birth to Eternity*

"Straight from a pastor's heart! The contents of this book will bring clarity and comfort to many who struggle with life's hardships. Willem Slomp writes as a man who knows God's Word and God's people. He also knows what it is to be in the crucible of suffering. Read what he has to say and rejoice with him as he dwells on the wonder of our gracious, wonderful and covenant keeping God and Saviour. Warmly recommended!"

>   --James Visscher, D.Min, Minister Emeritus, Langley Canadian Reformed Church

"This collection of erstwhile sermons is a heart-warming read. The overarching theme of God's covenantal faithfulness comes through in every topic that is discussed. The illustrations taken from the author's personal life and other sources are moving. In every chapter, one feels the heart of a shepherd who wants to give clear guidance and encouragement to his people."

>   -- Arjan de Visser, Th. Drs., Th. D., Professor of Ministry and Mission, Canadian Reformed Theological Seminary

"The first thing that strikes the reader about this collection of sermons is the deeply personal nature of each sermon. These are messages for real people striving to know the God of grace and how that works out in their own lives. The author does not avoid the difficult topics whether it is sin, dealing with grief and adversity, or coming closer to God through prayer. It is clear that Rev. Slomp is speaking from personal experience, including his own grief, struggles and joy. This makes his sermons resonate with the reader. Highly recommended."

>   --Richard Aasman, Minister Emeritus, Edmonton-Providence Canadian Reformed Church

Promises Unbroken

Exploring God's Covenant of Love from Birth to Eternity

Willem B. Slomp

Purple Breeze

PRESS

Purple Breeze Press, LLC

purplebreezepress.com

Promises Unbroken: Exploring God's Covenant of Love from Birth to Eternity

© 2024 Willem B. Slomp

Library of Congress Cataloguing in Publication Data

Names: Slomp, Willem B., author

Title: *Promises Unbroken: Exploring God's Covenant of Love from Birth to Eternity*

Description: First edition. | Purple Breeze Press, 2024

Library of Congress Control Number: 2024914084

ISBN Paperback: 979-8-9918895-0-6

Unless otherwise indicated, Scripture quotations are from the ESV (*The Holy Bible: English Standard Version*). (2016). Crossway Bibles.

Scripture quotations marked NIV84 are from the NIV (*The Holy Bible: New International Version*). (1984). Zondervan.

Scripture quotations marked NLT are from the NLT (*Holy Bible: New Living Translation*). (2015). Tyndale House Publishers.

Contents

Foreword

As its title suggests, this book is a love story.

What the book's title doesn't reveal is that it is a love story that functions on a number of levels.

The Story of God's Love

At the grandest level, this book tells the story of the gospel. My father often described the Bible to me as God's love story to his people. The sermons in this book were curated to tell that story in all its richness and wonder.

In many ways it is a simple love story.

God created the universe and all that is in it. He created humanity. He placed humanity at the center of that creation, in a beautiful garden that provided them with everything they needed. God walked in this garden with Adam and Eve because he created them to live in harmonious relationship with him. He gave them his perfect will and asked that in thankfulness for all he had done for them, all he had given them, they might honour that will.

But Adam and Eve rejected that will, despising God's gifts and his promise of eternal and perfect joy with him. Having broken their relationship with God, they hid from him. In response, God could have chosen to reject them and their offspring, to leave them—and us—in our brokenness and misery.

But God instead chose to seek them out. And having found them hiding in the garden, he chose to make them—and us—a promise: He would restore our broken relationship with him. He would again give us life. He would resurrect the promise of eternal joy and peace with him.

In Genesis 3:15, at the very beginning of the Bible, God makes this promise. How he would achieve this is only hinted at: an offspring of Adam would one day crush the serpent. Over several thousand years of revelation, God gradually made his action plan clearer: a sacrifice to pay for humanity's sins would have to be made; a son from the offspring of Judah, from the line of king David would be born; this child would set God's people free.

When Jesus Christ came into the world, he claimed to be that royal son. He also claimed to be the Son of God. He declared that he had come into the world to make the perfect sacrifice God demanded, to endure on our behalf what we could not: the wrath of God against sin. And on the cross, that is exactly what he did.

But while on earth, Jesus Christ also revealed that the promise of eternity is not for everyone; God reserves that promise only for those who believe in him, who acknowledge their brokenness and sin and their need for a Saviour; who recognize Jesus Christ as that Saviour. The amazing beauty of the gospel is that we do not—for we cannot—earn our salvation. It is a gift completely undeserved, entirely unearned. All God requires of us is what he required of Adam and Eve. Having received this gift, he calls us to follow his will, dedicating our lives to living in thankfulness to him.

The Bible is the story of underserved love. In the chapters of this book, my father retells this story, working out the details, explaining their significance, revealing through them what an amazing and wonderful God we have.

A Pastor's Love
On another level, this book is a love story about a pastor who dedicated his life to serving God and his people, to telling God's love story week in and week out from the pulpit. Reading the

sermons in this book brings back for me so many memories of conversations I have had with my father in his study, where he'd talk through with me his struggle to make this love story come alive from the pulpit. Every week he struggled with how he could reach each person in the pews before him. For more than thirty-five years he has honed this skill.

My father once told me that he preached as much for himself as he did for those in the pews. In the pages of this book, you also see the heart of a child of God. You see the heart of a pastor who knows his own sin, his own desperate need for a Saviour. You see the heart of a man who longs for the brokenness of this world to be mended, who looks forward to God's promised eternity. You see the heart of a man who knows the comfort and joy that comes from God, from trusting fully in the work of Jesus Christ, from knowing he has been redeemed, and from knowing that God's promised eternity is already his.

Several years ago, my father had open-heart surgery to replace a faulty valve. Complications from the surgery almost claimed his life. In his hospital room the day his doctors removed the breathing tube and lifted his sedation, I asked him if he had been afraid. His response: "Not everything from that time is clear in my mind, but I remember receiving the tremendous assurance that no matter what happens, whether life or death, everything will be okay. God spoke to me in my heart and assured me of eternal salvation."

In the pages of this book, you will see the heart of the man I have loved my whole life. A man who has taught me, both through his preaching and through how he lived, what it means to be a child of our loving God.

A Personal Love Story

This book is also a love story on a more personal level.

Throughout our lives, God places people in our paths who are a blessing to us. Some share our faith in Jesus Christ; others do not. The difficulty is that as we come to know them, we come to love them. They are good people. Kind. Generous. Warm. Gracious. Thoughtful. As we come to love them, we want to share eternity with them.

In this context, my conversations with my father as he crafted his sermons come to haunt me: how do you reach with the gospel the people you love?

My answer to this question has been through prayer to ask that God provide the means and the opportunity to do so.

Just over two years ago, my friend and mentor, Norbert Elliot, started Purple Breeze Press. Shortly after, he emailed me and asked if I thought my dad might be interested in publishing a book of sermons. I was immediately taken with this idea: an answer to my prayers.

When I pitched the book idea to my dad, I encouraged him to take it on. "If this book only reaches one person, and I could spend eternity with him," I said, "I would be forever grateful."

Over the past few years, I've cheered from the sidelines as two men I deeply love have collaborated on this book, honing and crafting the story it tells.

If you could have watched them work, you might have been struck with how deeply intellectual an exercise this has been. And in that you might stumble into an important paradox of the Christian faith. To believe in God, one must know God. In this way, Christianity is a deeply intellectual faith. But the paradox is this: while knowledge of God is necessary, knowledge does not save us. The intellectual must fuel an emotional response. We must fall in love with God. We must allow that love to transform us.

My hope is that the readers of this book will be taken in by the love stories it tells. I hope this book will deepen your understanding of who God is, of who Jesus Christ is, of what he has done for those who believe in him. I hope you will fall in love with him and be transformed for eternity.

David H Slomp, PhD
Professor
Associate Dean
Graduate Studies and Research, Faculty of Education
University of Lethbridge

Introduction:
The Many Blessings of God's
Covenant of Love

"One cannot capture the riches of the Bible in a single word. But if one merits consideration as a key concept in the Holy Scriptures, it is the word covenant.*"*

"God reveals himself from beginning to end in the Bible as the God of the covenant. It is by way of a covenant that he comes to us and enters into a relationship with us."

Clarence Stam (*The Covenant of Love*)

"And I will establish my covenant between me and you and your offspring after you throughout their generations for an everlasting covenant, to be God to you and to your offspring after you."

Genesis 17:7

When my son David approached me to write a book of sermons, I had my reservations. Many such books are already available from preachers and scholars who are much more capable than I am. What could I contribute?

However, he persisted and introduced me to his longtime colleague, Norbert Elliot. Together, they encouraged me to write

1

such a book, reminding me that as a father of seven children, grandfather of twenty-four grandchildren, and preacher and pastor for over thirty years, I have some distinctive experiences to share.

So I agreed, but I did not want this book to be like any other book of sermons. Instead, I wanted it to be more personal and accessible to a broader readership. I wanted it to deal with some of the pastoral and theological aspects of God's covenant of love and grace and how that informs us about who God's children are, how they become that way, and how that relationship with God is maintained.

The term "covenant" comes from Latin (*con venire*), meaning a coming together. It is one-sided in its establishment and two-sided in its existence. More simply stated, God established a relationship of love and faithfulness to which humankind must respond. It is a strong bond based on promises and demands in which both parties vow to fulfil their roles.

So, the focus of this book is on how God's covenant of grace provides the peace, hope, belonging, and security we so desperately need. The message of the covenant is powerful. It tells us, believers, that we belong to God, that he chose us despite our many moral and ethical failings, that he will be our strength in times of trouble, and that he has prepared a future for us that is beyond our wildest imaginations.

The apostle Paul's life serves as an excellent illustration. Paul experienced many trials and tribulations, and he identified himself as the worst of all sinners (1 Timothy 1:15). He experienced physical suffering, which included beatings, stoning, and imprisonment. At one point, he was left for dead. He endured shipwrecks and other dangers while travelling (2 Corinthians 11:23–27). He faced criticism, conflicts, and disagreements with others, as well as false accusations of not having the right qualifications for his position. He also was afflicted with a "thorn in the flesh," a source of torment he pleaded with God to remove (2 Corinthians 12:7–10). The weight of his sin, as evidenced by his statement, "Wretched man that I am," also at times led him to despair.

But it was the reality of God's covenantal love, fully expressed in Jesus Christ, that sustained him and filled him with contentment throughout his life and ministry. As he writes to the Philippians,

> Not that I am speaking of being in need, for I have
> learned in whatever situation I am to be content.
> I know how to be brought low, and I know how to
> abound. In any and every circumstance, I have
> learned the secret of facing plenty and hunger,
> abundance and need. I can do all things through him
> who strengthens me. (Philippians 4:11–13)

In my personal life and my vocation as a preacher and pastor, the biblical concept of the covenant has been an endless source of comfort, hope, joy, and strength. The deep love, care, and sense of belonging found in God through Jesus Christ have been the uniting thread throughout my ministry, my greatest inspiration, and my deepest comfort in my personal trials. I could share many examples from my life and ministry, but four brief stories will suffice.

A Story of Love

I grew up in the Netherlands with two sisters, one older and one younger, and parents who loved us and each other. Above all, they loved the Lord and were very serious about their faith. It was not a perfect family—there is no such thing. But to my father, it was very important to keep your promises. He held fast to the Dutch adage *Belofte maakt schuld* ("A promise made is a debt unpaid").

Those three words still ring in my ears, for they are covenantal words. They are words upon which relationships are established and maintained. That is what God did when he made a covenant with us and told us that he is our God who loves us and who will never forsake us. This held true even after the fall into sin (see Chapters 1 and 2), and he promised additionally that if we held on to him in faith, he would forgive us our sins and give us eternal life.

My parents were faithful to their wedding vows through sixty-seven years of marriage and loved each other dearly, but their marriage was not without struggles. As he got older, my father's disposition began to change because he experienced his body deteriorating. Fading eyesight and increasing deafness weighed heavily on him. Growing old was difficult for him. He was less patient with my sweet mother and, for a while, made life hard for her.

During a visit, she confided in me, expressing her deep sadness due to his treatment of her. However, sometime later, I noticed a remarkable shift in her mood. Curious, I asked her if my father had changed. Her response surprised me: "No," she said, "I changed." She didn't tell me how she changed, but I noticed that she went back to her old self, being joyful and kind. She changed her attitude. My dad, in turn, also changed his disposition for the better.

My mother grew up belonging to a church where she was made to doubt her salvation, which greatly grieved her. After searching the Bible and discussing this extensively with her husband-to-be (my dad), she learned to trust God's Word that you are saved through faith alone and that you do not need a separate message of God to assure you. God's wonderful promises in the Bible are enough (e.g., John 3:16).

When she died at the age of ninety-four, I inherited her Bible, which was full of notations, underlining, and highlights. She knew her Bible and, through a lifetime of meditation upon it, had deepened her understanding of God's covenantal love and its implications for her life. She knew God's eternal and undeserved love personally. And in thankfulness, she gave that same eternal and undeserved love to my father.

A Story of Sin and Evil

The most wonderful promise of the covenant is that God will save us from sin and death. But what does that mean? Without understanding its implications, we remain unaware of our need for deliverance. In today's world, discussions about sin and evil are scarce. While individual sins are often addressed within Christian circles, the pervasive evil that surrounds us and our complicity in it receives less attention.

The older I get, the more I realize how little insight I have into my personal sinfulness. By nature, we human beings make ourselves into little gods, applying everything that happens around us to ourselves first before we think about the Almighty God and others. In his work *Institutes of the Christian Religion (I.11.8)*, John Calvin famously wrote, "Man's nature, so to speak, is a perpetual factory of idols." Calvin recognized that the human mind is often filled with pride and arrogance, thinking that *we* are the centre of the universe and that God is out of the picture.

The fact is, however, that God is real, and we are totally dependent on him, not only for our well-being and salvation, but for our very existence. Without God, we are nothing, and we have nothing.

The apostle Paul writes that we should not think of ourselves

5

"more highly than we ought" (Romans 12:3). Humility before God and others is paramount.

So, as I prepare my sermons, I always strive to ensure that I do not come across as someone who has it all together. I want the people in the pews to see me as one of them. I want them to know that I, too, am a sinner and have faced similar struggles. (See Chapter 2 for a discussion of how prone we are to temptation and how we, because of Jesus's love and perfect obedience, can be delivered from evil.)

A Story of Care

As a pastor, I have been at many deathbeds and seen much grief. In such circumstances, it is a great blessing to experience the comfort of God's covenantal faithfulness and care. If there is one thing that people need amid suffering, uncertainty, and grief, it is comfort. When someone is diagnosed with a serious illness, much chaos and uncertainty ensue. What is the prognosis? Is it terminal? Will he or she survive or be permanently debilitated? Will he or she be able to cope with the shock and pain of it all? One's mind goes a mile a minute. There is so much uncertainty and anxiety. It can be overwhelming.

I personally experienced this in June 2017, when our youngest son, Stephen, husband and father of three little boys, became a mute quadriplegic at the age of twenty-eight, having been afflicted with Acute Disseminated Encephalomyelitis (ADEM), a neurological disease of the brain (see the introduction to Chapter 9). I will never forget the sheer agony I experienced when the neurologist came into the room I was in with my wonderful daughter-in-law and told us about Stephen's devastating prognosis. It hit us like a ton of bricks. We embraced and cried our eyes out. When I called my oldest daughter with the distressing news, I could not get the words out. All she could hear was me sobbing at the other end of the phone. And so she asked in alarm, "Dad, what's wrong, what's wrong? Speak to me. . . ."

Stephen remained in the hospital for more than half a year, and during that time, I drew tremendous comfort from my wife, children, and grandchildren and from many members of the church. Above all, I drew comfort from God's Word and his sure and wonderful covenantal promises.

As we gathered as family and friends in the hospital's atrium, we frequently sang songs from the *Book of Praise* around the piano. Psalm 42:3 is one of my favourites:

> *O my soul, why are you grieving,*
> *why disquieted in me?*
> *Put your hope in God, believing*
> *he will still your refuge be.*
> *I again shall see his face*
> *and extol him for his grace.*
> *He will show his help and favour,*
> *for he is my God and Saviour.*

It has now been seven years. Although Stephen understands everything that is said to him, he is unable to communicate and make his needs known. My wife, Barb, consequently visits Stephen daily in his long-term care facility. His wife and three children, his siblings and their spouses, nieces and nephews, uncles and aunts, and members of the church also regularly visit him. The men of the church regularly hold Bible study meetings in his long-term care facility so that he, too, can participate by listening in.

A Story of Belonging

What a profound blessing it is to have family, friends, and the church community by one's side, providing comfort and support. My wife, who has been my unwavering companion for over half a century, has been and is a beacon of love and wisdom. Without her, I would have been lost. I wholeheartedly thank God for her steadfast support.

My children are more than mere offspring—they are my cherished friends and confidants. Each brings a unique perspective. Their love and counsel are precious beyond measure.

Additionally, I hold in high esteem the elders and deacons of the churches I've served. Their sage advice, steady guidance, and uplifting encouragement have been invaluable.

We need each other for comfort, instruction, and companionship. Yet so many people go it alone, which makes life difficult and almost impossible.

The power of a supportive community is paramount. This was especially brought home to me a few years ago when I made a presentation to the Edmonton Autism Society. Our second youngest son was born with a condition known as Prader-Willi Syndrome (PWS), which is a complex genetic disorder characterized by several features, including intellectual disabilities, compulsive behaviours, and hyperphagia (an insatiable appetite leading to obesity). It is considered to be part of the autism spectrum.

Our son needs 24/7 supervision. He now lives in his own apartment and has his own caregivers. To make this all happen, we needed help. And so we approached church members and others who have shown interest in him to help us set up a micro-board. To make a long story short, we successfully approached the provincial government for funding. We continue to receive help

8

with the administration of the funds and the management of staff.

Others in similar circumstances wanted to do the same, so I was invited to an autism support group. About fifty people were in attendance, and in my naivety, I told them that they should start the way I started, by inviting people to help them set up a friendship society of friends and relatives. It quickly became apparent that many of them did not have any support group around them at all. One lady told me, "I have no family here, and I do not have anybody to help me. My autistic son is at home with me, and he is in his room day in and day out, except one evening when he goes to see his counsellor." Others came with similar stories.

I was struck by their sense of despair and isolation and realized that many people in today's world are lonely and depressed. This made me appreciate all the more what a blessing it is to belong to a community that cares about others, and it motivated me to be more involved in outreach to the community.

We need others to lean on for support and friendship. Above all, we need God to comfort and guide us and to include us as part of his family. That is what God provides in his covenantal love.

Note on the Heidelberg Catechism

As readers will see, I reference the Heidelberg Catechism throughout this book. A note on it here may be useful.

In Reformed churches, it's common to regularly preach and teach from a confession called the Heidelberg Catechism. This Catechism was first published in 1563 and is considered the most influential among several catechisms from the Reformation period. It condenses the main teachings of the Bible into fifty-two sections, called Lord's Days, with a total of 129 questions and answers. Initially, it was meant for educating young people, but soon it became a tool for teaching the entire congregation. Each Lord's Day serves as a basis for the afternoon sermon, while in the morning, a text from the Bible is typically used. Some people criticize this approach because they believe every sermon should directly come from the Bible rather than from a human-made document. However, Reformed churches argue that the Catechism accurately summarizes the teachings of the Bible, as evidenced by the many Bible references provided with each question and answer. Using the Catechism also ensures that all the Bible's teachings are covered at least once a year, preventing preachers from fixating on their personal interests or preferences.

Overview

Although each chapter in this book stands on its own and can be read as such, the book has a flow and an overarching theme. The book begins where it all started, with creation, while keeping in mind our current perspective—our sinful, broken situation. The perfect relationship with God became defective when humankind rebelled against him. There were all kinds of detrimental ramifications which made us afraid and anxious. But although we changed, God did not and remains on his throne. Therefore, we should always trust in him and be at peace.

Chapter 2 describes the fall into sin, how it happened, and why sin continues to happen. There, we learn about the tricks of the devil, how we fell for those tricks in Paradise, and how we fall for his tricks repeatedly today. Yet, despite this, God continues to engage us and wants to be in a relationship with us.

Chapters 3 and 4 introduce circumcision and baptism, the Old and New Testament signs and seals of the covenant. They testify to God's faithfulness to his children from the cradle to the grave and into eternity. Chapter 5 gives us a picture of how we become part of God's family and how, in the final analysis, it is all God's doing.

Chapters 6, 7, and 8 discuss the importance of belonging together in one's earthly home, one's spiritual home, and one's eternal home. There, we see that God loves all kinds of people, regardless of their colour, their ethnic background, their past, or anything else that makes them different. God makes no distinctions and loves his children unconditionally, as should we.

Chapters 9, 10, and 11 teach us about grief and sorrow and how to trust in God in all circumstances. These chapters were very therapeutic to me in so many ways, and I hope and pray that the reader will also derive comfort from them.

Chapter 12 teaches us about how we connect with God through prayer and how that brings us closer to him. It is the most intimate form of communication that directly connects us to God on a personal level.

I hope that through reading this book, you will gain a deeper knowledge of God's love, as expressed so beautifully in the covenant, and that this knowledge will provide you, as it has done for me, with the strength to "press on toward the goal for the prize of the upward call of God in Christ Jesus" (Philippians 3:14).

Chapter 1
God As Creator and Guide

"Let all the earth fear the LORD;
let all the inhabitants of the world stand in awe of him!
For he spoke, and it came to be;
he commanded, and it stood firm."
Psalm 33:8–9

Introduction

In ancient Greek and Roman theatre, there was an interesting idea called "deus ex machina." This meant a surprising twist where a god or unexpected force suddenly appeared to solve a problem that seemed impossible to fix. In this theatrical technique, a "god" would be hung above the stage in Greek or Roman theater. This character would help explain a mystery and move the story forward.

This is also how creation myths came into existence. They are stories that explain how the world and humanity came into existence. They often involve gods or supernatural beings and reflect the values and beliefs of the cultures that created them. These myths can describe the creation of the earth, the sky, animals, and humans, and often address themes like chaos, order, and the relationship between humans and the divine. Each myth offers insights into how ancient people understood their place in the world. The gods revealed in these narratives, however, are often as flawed and capricious as the storytellers who wove them into existence. Often, they reflect and amplify both the good and the brokenness in the cultures they inhabited, while at the same time, they provided an anchor for that culture and that community, a place from which to build. Rather than attributing the magnificent, beautiful, and intricate creation to the Almighty God, as revealed in all of creation and in God's Word, storytellers often ascribe the existence of the world and its inhabitants to the capricious actions of diverse gods and goddesses.

The divinely inspired apostle Paul explains how these flawed visions came about. He writes,

> For although they knew God, they did not honor
> him as God or give thanks to him, but they became
> futile in their thinking, and their foolish hearts
> were darkened. Claiming to be wise, they became
> fools, and exchanged the glory of the immortal God
> for images resembling mortal man and birds and
> animals and creeping things. (Romans. 1:21–23)

In post-enlightenment culture, the theory of evolution was created by those who wanted an alternative to the biblical creation story. Like all origin stories, the theory provides an explanation for how we came to be, reflects the culture in which it originated, provides a means for explaining the present, and points to the conflicts and solutions of the future. It begins with chaos; is driven by the vagaries of chance, randomness, and cruel nature; and constructs a society that is fearful of these very things. In evolutionary theory, we have replaced the vagaries of flawed and capricious gods with the even greater instability wrought by a foundation of chaos and chance. To survive, we must be the fittest of creeping things.

The gospel of Jesus Christ, however, offers an origin story unlike any other. It begins with a perfect God, it begins with a perfect love, it begins with a perfect will. That almighty God, who exists in three persons—Father, Son, and Holy Spirit—created, out of nothing, a human species cast in his image; he placed that species in a world of his making, and he placed that world in a universe of his creation. Having created humanity, God gave them his perfect will.

When humanity rebelled against that perfect will, we brought brokenness, chaos, and conflict into this perfect creation. In response to that betrayal, God exercised his perfect love. He did not watch to see who survived. Instead, he loved.

The exercising of God's perfect love in a world broken by human betrayal is the story of the Bible. It explains—better than any other origin story—our current condition, it reveals with perfect vision the struggles of the future, and it points to the only perfect ending: a permanent solution to the pain and suffering, the brokenness and the sorrow, the chaos and the uncertainty we all suffer through.

There are many beautiful passages in the Scriptures that teach us about God's beautiful creation and our place in it. Psalm 104 is one of those, and I use it, along with the Heidelberg Catechism (See Introduction), to support this most essential and profound doctrine.

In this chapter, I introduce you to this perfect God and his perfect love.

Scripture

Psalm 104:1–35

1 Bless the LORD, O my soul! O LORD my God, you are very great! You are clothed with splendor and majesty,

2 covering yourself with light as with a garment, stretching out the heavens like a tent.

3 He lays the beams of his chambers on the waters; he makes the clouds his chariot; he rides on the wings of the wind;

4 he makes his messengers winds, his ministers a flaming fire.

5 He set the earth on its foundations, so that it should never be moved.

6 You covered it with the deep as with a garment; the waters stood above the mountains.

7 At your rebuke they fled; at the sound of your thunder they took to flight.

8 The mountains rose, the valleys sank down to the place that you appointed for them.

9 You set a boundary that they may not pass, so that they might not again cover the earth.

10 You make springs gush forth in the valleys; they flow between the hills;

11 they give drink to every beast of the field; the wild donkeys quench their thirst.

12 Beside them the birds of the heavens dwell; they sing among the branches.

13 From your lofty abode you water the mountains; the earth is satisfied with the fruit of your work.

14 You cause the grass to grow for the livestock and plants for man to cultivate, that he may bring forth food from the earth

15 and wine to gladden the heart of man, oil to make his face shine and bread to strengthen man's heart.

16 The trees of the LORD are watered abundantly, the

15

cedars of Lebanon that he planted.

17 In them the birds build their nests; the stork has her home in the fir trees.

18 The high mountains are for the wild goats; the rocks are a refuge for the rock badgers.

19 He made the moon to mark the seasons; the sun knows its time for setting.

20 You make darkness, and it is night, when all the beasts of the forest creep about.

21 The young lions roar for their prey, seeking their food from God.

22 When the sun rises, they steal away and lie down in their dens.

23 Man goes out to his work and to his labor until the evening.

24 O Lord, how manifold are your works! In wisdom have you made them all; the earth is full of your creatures.

25 Here is the sea, great and wide, which teems with creatures innumerable, living things both small and great.

26 There go the ships, and Leviathan, which you formed to play in it.

27 These all look to you, to give them their food in due season.

28 When you give it to them, they gather it up; when you open your hand, they are filled with good things.

29 When you hide your face, they are dismayed; when you take away their breath, they die and return to their dust.

30 When you send forth your Spirit, they are created, and you renew the face of the ground.

31 May the glory of the LORD endure forever; may the LORD rejoice in his works,

32 who looks on the earth and it trembles, who touches the mountains and they smoke!

33 I will sing to the LORD as long as I live; I will sing praise to my God while I have being.

34 May my meditation be pleasing to him, for I rejoice in the LORD.

35 Let sinners be consumed from the earth, and let the wicked be no more! Bless the LORD, O my soul! Praise the LORD!

Heidelberg Catechism

26.   Q. What do you believe when you say:
       I believe in God the Father almighty,
       Creator of heaven and earth?

      A. That the eternal Father of our Lord Jesus Christ,
         who out of nothing created heaven and earth
         and all that is in them,[1]
         and who still upholds and governs them
         by his eternal counsel and providence,[2]
         is, for the sake of Christ his Son,
         my God and my Father.[3]

         In him I trust so completely
         as to have no doubt
         that he will provide me
         with all things necessary for body and soul,[4]
         and will also turn to my good
         whatever adversity he sends me
         in this life of sorrow.[5]

         He is able to do so as almighty God,[6]
         and willing also as a faithful Father.[7]

[1] Gen 1 and 2; Ex 20:11; Job 38 and 39; Ps 33:6; Is 44:24; Acts 4:24; 14:15.
[2] Ps 104:27–30; Mt 6:30; 10:29; Eph 1:11.
[3] Jn 1:12, 13; Rom 8:15, 16; Gal 4:4–7; Eph 1:5.
[4] Ps 55:22; Mt 6:25, 26; Lk 12:22–31.
[5] Rom 8:28.
[6] Gen 18:14; Rom 8:31–39.
[7] Mt 6:32, 33; 7:9–11.

The Controlling Guide to Our Destination

I remember some time ago, as I sat on a plane about to take off, looking out the window on one side of the plane. That side showed a beautiful sunset. You could see the sky's various colours as the sun sank below the horizon. From that perspective, everything looked peaceful and serene. But as I looked through the window on the other side of the plane, I saw a completely different picture. I saw angry, gathering clouds, grey and black, and knew that a storm was about to unleash its fury.

Beside me was a woman who obviously was nervous about flying. She kept looking out of that one side of the plane that showed the gloomy and threatening weather. As we took off, she continued to look out of that side of the plane, becoming more and more nervous. It didn't help that right after takeoff, the ride was bumpy for a time as well.

I thought to myself, why doesn't she look out the other side of the plane? She would feel much less anxious. For we are all on the same plane, including the pilot, and we will all go to the same destination. The pilot knows what he is doing. He wouldn't take off if it weren't safe.

I also thought to myself, isn't that the way it is with life as well? As Christians, we all go to the same destination as we make our way through life. But, as we make our way through life, we sometimes look out the wrong window. Some people do it all the time.

Perhaps you do that regularly. So, let me ask you, is your life full of anxiety and tension? Do you constantly look at all the things that can and do sometimes go wrong? Are you scared when things get a little bit bumpy?

Well, then change your view. Look out of the other window.

Look at God's creation and notice how wonderfully he has made it. There's immense beauty in God's creation. Through your eyes of faith, you can see that only an Almighty God could create something as beautiful and intricate as he and that only that Almighty God can control our destiny.

It is true that, because of sin this creation is also full of dangers. There are earthquakes. Floods. Hurricanes and tornadoes. Ice storms. Things break down and fall and deteriorate. Unexpected things can happen to you personally. You can lose your health and your possessions. A lot of bad things can happen.

But, let's not forget that we, as believers, are all going to the same destination. And the same pilot is in control, which is the Lord God himself. And he wants you to trust in him. He has created the vessel you travel on, this whole earth, the entire universe. You can safely put your life into his hands.

In this chapter, we will see that our faithful Father is the Almighty Creator who safely guides us to our destination. We will see that we know this, first by carefully observing the miracles of his creation, and secondly by trusting his ability and willingness to guide us to our destination.

The Miracle of God's Creation

Lord's Day 9 of the Heidelberg Catechism deals with the first article of the Apostle's Creed and begins where the Bible also begins, namely with our creation. You would expect, therefore, that this Lord's Day would address some of the problems people have concerning creation, for example, the fact that God created all things in six days and that it did not come about through any other means. You would expect the emphasis to be on the Almighty Creator and what he is all able to do.

However, that is not the case. The emphasis is not first on God the Creator but on God as the eternal Father of our Lord Jesus Christ, who is also my Father.

Indeed, creation is mentioned in this Lord's Day, but the main point is that "the eternal Father of our Lord Jesus Christ . . . is also my God and Father." He created this world for his children, for us.

That is also how you must see Genesis 1. In the first chapter of the Bible, we get the diary of our Lord God, wherein he describes how he lovingly prepared a wonderful home for us. It is a home which has as its roof the changing cloud formations, and the sun for central heat, acting as a permanent light. It also has the moon and the stars that light up the sky at night. The home has various kinds of carpets: grass, trees, and plants. It has mountains and valleys. The cupboards of the house are full. There is fruit on the trees, wheat and barley in the fields, and plenty to eat. The Lord God also put the animals on the earth for man to play with and delight in.

He prepared the earth lovingly, like a father and mother do when they expect a child. They select a bedroom close to their own so that they can be there whenever the child needs them. They put everything there that the baby could need: a soft warm bed, a changing table, toys, and restful wallpaper. When everything is ready, the baby can come.

That is how God prepared the earth for all of us. He made everything ready for his children, Adam and Eve, and their offspring. God created them in his image. The man and the woman were created to be different from all the other creatures in that they would be his covenant children. Adam and Eve and their offspring would inherit the whole earth. God intended that his children would live in that home happily and contented forever.

And he would be close to them; he would be next door. They could call upon him at any time.

The author of Psalm 104 greatly appreciated the home that God created for him. He sees the hand of his heavenly Father in everything. He observes God's wonderful creation around him and views his surroundings as the radiant and stately robe with which the invisible Creator has clothed himself to display his glory.

He looked around and stood in awe of the beauty in the sky, the shifting clouds and the sun's rays. He felt the sand at the seashore between his toes and the cool water as it lapped against his legs; how the waters of the seas are kept within their boundaries. The waters can only go so far, and then they return to where they came. He looked at the raging rivers and how they flowed between the mountains. He saw how beautifully God made everything, and how the waters served to quench the thirst of all kinds of animals, the birds and the beasts of the field and the wild donkeys.

And when he heard the roaring of a lion, he perceived that as the lion asking for his food from God. He saw God's hand in all of creation. When he heard the thunder, he heard the voice of God. He stood in awe of how the birds make their nests and how the stork makes a home in the pine trees. He was excited by how everything happened with seasonal regularity. There's the rhythm of light and darkness, spring, summer, autumn, and winter.

As the psalmist observed all these things, he did not, as modern man does, speak about "Mother Earth" or "the laws of nature." He did not give credit to an impersonal intelligent design either. No, he praises God: "Praise the LORD, O my soul. Oh LORD my God, you are very great" (vs.1).

He perceived the Father's breath in the winds. He did not say, "Oh, how the wind blows." But he said, look at how the Father uses the wind as his messenger (vs.4). And when the sun rises, he did not just marvel at that miracle, but he marvelled at his heavenly Father who caused this to happen. In everything he saw his heavenly Father as the Almighty Creator who upholds and governs all things.

Is that how you also see this world? Do you stand in awe daily of the work of creation of your heavenly Father? Do you see the hand of your heavenly Father when the first snow falls out of the sky? Do you see the miracle of each snowflake? Unlike man-made snow, there is not one snowflake falling from the sky that is the same as the other. That's God's doing.

Do you see the miracle in a house plant as it unfolds its leaves and produces flowers? Do you hear the birds singing and see the beauty of it all? How God created that bird, and how he provides for him every day, making sure that he has food and drink?

It is absolutely marvellous the way God has created things. Humankind continues to discover more and more. That is because God created the earth so beautifully with so many elements that innumerable new things are ready to be discovered.

Think about what has been discovered in the past century. Man discovered that he could communicate through radio waves and telephone lines. Man discovered how he could harness steam powerful enough to push a locomotive along rail lines. Man discovered electricity. Man discovered flight. He even discovered that he could fly to the moon. He discovered the computer chip. And so the list can go on and on.

There are so many more things yet to be discovered. God put it all there for his glory and for us to discover and enjoy. And we have only scratched the surface.

Why did he make these things? He gave them to us to satisfy

our curiosity, and to keep us busy. He gave them to us to exercise our cultural mandate. He made them for us to discover them, so that we could give glory to God, just as the psalmist does. God wants us to use his creation to his glory, and to stand in awe of it.

I once read a story about a father and a little boy that struck me. The father was busy at work on his desk by the window, oblivious to his surroundings. And then he heard the banging and the clanging of a garbage truck. And he looked outside. He saw his four-year-old son sitting on the curb watching in awe and wonder as that great big garbage truck picked up the garbage in its steel claws and then gobbled it up. The boy's eyes almost popped out of his head.

The father saw how awe-struck and mesmerized his little boy was by the mechanics of it all. You and I are used to these kinds of things. If we were to come upon a garbage truck, we would barely give it a glance as we pass by. A truck is just a man-made thing and ultimately is not very complicated. But to that little boy, that garbage truck was awesome. We pass by so many things. We take so many things for granted.

It would be good to go back to that time in our lives when we stood in awe of everything around us. God's creation is truly awesome.

The Scriptures often speak about the hands of God. God, of course, doesn't have hands like we do. It is a figure of speech. We use such figures of speech for ourselves as well. When we have control of a situation, for example, then we will say that we have everything in hand. And now the same thing is true of God regarding creation. He holds it, as it were, in his hand. And so, he can shape it and do with it whatever he wants. He is in complete control of it all.

There are many things we are not able to hold in our hands. And that is because we are not strong enough. We cannot hold a mountain or a tree in our hand. And we cannot control all situations. Those things are impossible for us to be able to do.

But God's power is such that he can hold all of creation in his hand. He can hold on to the whole earth. He can hold billions upon billions of stars in his hand as well. And whatever may come along, whatever may happen, the situation never gets out of hand. There is no limit to what God can do. He is that powerful. He is that wise.

But what does it mean that he upholds it? We should not think that that is all God does. That is how some people picture it. They think of God as an artist, a sculptor, who, when finished with his creation, puts his sculpture somewhere so that he and others can look at it and admire it.

God, however, does not do that. He does not just put his creation somewhere for him to gaze at and marvel at. He does not leave it just in his hand either, so all he does is move it so that he can look at it from all angles. No, God is always busy with his creation. He continues to mould and shape his creation. He is always busy with his hands. His hands are never idle.

That is quite clear from Psalm 104. That psalm describes how God is responsible not only for putting the earth on its foundations, as it says in verse 5, but also for making the springs gush forth in the valleys, and for giving drink to every beast of the field, and for giving the birds their habitations. He is the one who causes the grass to grow for the cattle and plants for man to cultivate. He is the one who waters the trees so that they can grow and so that the birds can build their nests in them. He is also the one who made the moon to mark the seasons, as it says in verse 19. And he is the one who, as the catechism says, "still upholds and governs them by his eternal counsel and providence."

But do you know what is so incredibly wonderful? He takes care especially of us. Having been made in God's image, we are the crown of his creation. We are very special to him. The catechism also tells us that he governs his creation, including all the creatures. He governs them; he rules them; he directs their lives.

You can only do that if you have a specific goal in mind. And God does. Everything that happens here on earth with his creatures is directed towards a particular goal. The world is unlike a stationary automobile with its engine running in neutral. No, it is going places. It is on the way to somewhere. And God has determined its destination. Nothing and no one can prevent God from realizing the goal that he has set for his creation.

God Guides Us to Our Final Destination

Did you ever consider that it is a miracle that this world still turns and that many good things still do happen? Because of our sin, creation is spoiled. We have allowed the devil to reign this world, our hearts, our flesh. Is it not a miracle that this world is still in existence? That God did not destroy everything? Is it not a miracle that every day babies are still being born? Is it not a miracle that the sun shines every day and that creation is being preserved as it is?

These miracles happen only because of one thing: the Lord Jesus Christ came to redeem this world. He makes it possible that we can be alive physically and eternally. He makes it possible that we have food on our table and a roof over our heads and that we have clothes. He makes it possible that we can gather together in church every Sunday. He makes it possible that we can have jobs to keep us busy. He makes it possible that we can enjoy the many good things.

Oh sure, there is pain and sorrow here on this earth. There are many disappointments. But concentrate on something other than those things and look out of the right window. God never left the driver's seat. He is still there, bringing this whole world to its final destination. Nothing can change that.

Think about the miracle that you are alive and that you have hope because of the Lord Jesus Christ. You have great hope for the future. The Lord God tells you that nothing can separate you from his love. And if that's what you concentrate on, then you can also withstand the bumps and grinds of life. As the catechism says, he is able to do everything as Almighty God, but he is willing to do that also because he is our heavenly Father.

Our confession says, "I trust in him so completely as to have no doubt that he will provide me with all things necessary for body and soul and will also turn to my good whatever adversity he sends me in his life of sorrow." That's our beautiful and comforting confession. To trust in him is to know him.

How do you know him? You know him from creation all around you, but especially from his Word. God wants us to acknowledge that he is always in control, also when bad things happen.

When you don't believe, you will be full of anxiety. You will be afraid when the economy deteriorates, or you become seriously ill. Without trusting in God, you will not feel in control. You are set adrift if you don't acknowledge God as your heavenly Father and don't believe in him. Without faith, you will not make it to your final destination with your heavenly Father.

Please note that Psalm 104 ends with a curse. After describing God's wonderful creation, the psalmist says, "Let sinners be consumed from the earth, and let the wicked be no more!"

Do you know why? Because God wants a world without sin and pain. He has us looking forward to the new earth where the gathering of stormy clouds will no longer happen. Where our trials and tribulations will be over and where there will be peace and solitude.

In the end, there is no room for those who do not acknowledge that our heavenly Father is the Creator of all things and that he is the One who also preserves all things. He is the One who loves you so much that he gave his only Son so that this world as we now know it can be renewed, totally renewed. And you had better acknowledge that now, or God will not acknowledge you as his child.

For that reason, he adds once again, "Bless the LORD, O my soul! Praise the LORD!" There is much reason to praise him, for he is going to do away with wickedness and sin on this earth. That is why he sent his Son. He sent his Son to do away with sin. He sent his Son because he loves us so much that never again do we have to experience sin and misery.

And so, don't look out of the wrong window and at the dark and gloomy side of life; don't be anxious and afraid. But look at the beauty of all of God's creation. And trust in the Almighty God. And he will bring you to your final destination safe and sound. Don't worry. Trust in him. As the catechism says, "He is able to do so as almighty God, and willing also as a faithful Father."

Reflection

1. Consider the various factors that contribute to your anxiety and identify the specific triggers for these feelings. Then, reflect on how the beauty and complexity inherent in God's creation serve as a source of comfort. How does God's creation—in all its beauty and complexity—prevent you from succumbing to anxiety?

2. In Psalm 104:23–24, we read that "Man goes out to his work and to his labor until the evening. O LORD, how manifold are your works! In wisdom have you made them all." In the daily journey of life, we encounter both highs and lows. How does God utilize these experiences so that, each day, we ensure that we allow God to lead us toward our ultimate destination?

Chapter 2
Sin, Temptation, and God's Love

"Let no one say when he is tempted,
'I am being tempted by God,'
for God cannot be tempted with evil,
and he himself tempts no one.
But each person is tempted when he is lured and
enticed by his own desire.
Then desire when it has conceived gives birth to sin,
and sin when it is fully grown brings forth death."

James 1:13–15

"For we do not have a high priest
who is unable to sympathize with our weaknesses, but
one who in every respect has been tempted as we are,
yet without sin."

Hebrews 4:15

Introduction

The Christian faith is like no other. It is the only religion in the world that teaches that we are totally dependent on God for everything. Christianity was not established by a prophet to help you find God, as other religions (such as Islam) teach, but by a true prophet, Jesus Christ, who is both God and man and who, because of his great love, leads you to God. As that true prophet, Jesus Christ, says in John 6:44, "No one can come to me unless the Father who sent me draws him. And I will raise him up on the last day."

Without him seeking us, we cannot find God, and we cannot save ourselves either. We also cannot earn salvation by doing the right things or following the right path. The Bible teaches that we have no worthy qualities that make us acceptable to God. Salvation is a gift from God. As we read in Ephesians 2:8–9, "For by grace you have been saved through faith. And this is not your own doing; it is the gift of God, not a result of works, so that no one may boast."

But what has happened that made us need that gift of faith? How did we lose the connection with God? For we cannot see him. And why and from what do we need to be saved? How did pain and suffering come about?

To understand this, we must examine the events in the Garden of Eden, where humanity fell into sin. After creation, God intended for mankind to exist in a loving relationship with him. Tragically, this relationship became broken. Genesis 3 explains how the serpent led Adam and Eve astray, enticing them to pursue their selfish desires. They chose to heed the devil rather than God, and as a result, they brought upon themselves the curse of God, leading to suffering, death, conflict, and pain.

How could such consequences occur if God is loving and perfect? This question poses a significant challenge for many in understanding Christianity. Love is intertwined with the concept of free choice and its consequences. If we were created as preprogrammed computers or puppets without a free will, we would not possess the capacity for genuine love. Such a creature would lack purpose and worth. True love necessitates the freedom to choose. Without choice, we would be nothing more than cold, remotely controlled robots. What would be the purpose or worth of such a creature?

In Paradise, Adam and Eve, having been tempted by the devil, made the wrong choices, and consequently, our human nature became corrupted (Romans 5:12). Nevertheless, God still wants us to make the right choices and resist the temptation to sin. That is why we need to be aware of how the devil tempts us and tries to have us obey him rather than God.

This chapter also addresses the temptation of Jesus, as recorded in Matthew 4. Only by considering how Jesus, our Lord and Saviour, faced and overcame the temptations of the devil, can we be saved from our inclination to repeatedly succumb to the devil's wicked schemes. We must follow his example and do our utmost to obey God.

Thankfully, Jesus is more than an example to us: he actually fulfils the law for us. Only through faith in him can we be declared innocent and accepted in the sight of God. And in thankfulness to God, we must do our utmost not to be led into temptation.

As you read this chapter, I invite you to consider how prone we are to temptation and how we, through God's love in Jesus Christ, can be delivered from the evil one.

Scripture

Genesis 2:15–18

The Forbidden Fruit

15 The Lord God took the man and put him in the garden of Eden to work it and keep it.

16 And the Lord God commanded the man, saying, "You may surely eat of every tree of the garden,

17 but of the tree of the knowledge of good and evil you shall not eat, for in the day that you eat of it you shall surely die."

18 Then the Lord God said, "It is not good that the man should be alone; I will make him a helper fit for him."

Genesis 3:1–6

The Temptation of Adam and Eve

3 Now the serpent was more crafty than any other beast of the field that the Lord God had made.

He said to the woman, "Did God actually say, 'You shall not eat of any tree in the garden'?"

2 And the woman said to the serpent, "We may eat of the fruit of the trees in the garden,

3 but God said, 'You shall not eat of the fruit of the tree that is in the midst of the garden, neither shall you touch it, lest you die.' "

4 But the serpent said to the woman, "You will not surely die.

5 For God knows that when you eat of it your eyes will be opened, and you will be like God, knowing good and evil."

6 So when the woman saw that the tree was good for food, and that it was a delight to the eyes, and that the tree was to be desired to make one wise, she took of its fruit and ate, and she also gave some to her husband who was with her, and he ate.

Matthew 4:1–11

The Temptation of Jesus

4 Then Jesus was led up by the Spirit into the wilderness to be tempted by the devil.

2 And after fasting forty days and forty nights, he was hungry.

3 And the tempter came and said to him, "If you are the Son of God, command these stones to become loaves of bread."

4 But he answered, "It is written,

'Man shall not live by bread alone, but by every word that comes from the mouth of God.' "

5 Then the devil took him to the holy city and set him on the pinnacle of the temple

6 and said to him, "If you are the Son of God, throw yourself down, for it is written,

'He will command his angels concerning you,'

and 'On their hands they will bear you up,

lest you strike your foot against a stone.'"

7 Jesus said to him, "Again it is written, 'You shall not put the Lord your God to the test.'"

8 Again, the devil took him to a very high mountain and showed him all the kingdoms of the world and their glory.

9 And he said to him, "All these I will give you, if you will fall down and worship me."

10 Then Jesus said to him, "Be gone, Satan! For it is written,

'You shall worship the Lord your God and him only shall you serve.'"

11 Then the devil left him, and behold, angels came and were ministering to him.

Heidelberg Catechism

8.   Q. But are we so corrupt
        that we are totally unable to do any good
        and inclined to all evil?

     A. Yes,[1] unless we are regenerated
        by the Spirit of God.[2]

[1] Gen 6:5; 8:21; Job 14:4; Is 53:6.
[2] Jn 3:3–5.

Our Common Weaknesses

Have you ever been deeply disappointed in someone whom you held in high regard for a long time and who did something unthinkable? You never imagined that this person would do such a thing. Someone dear was caught in some secret sin and afterwards went from bad to worse.

A husband and father, or a wife and mother, a guardian or loved one does something unimaginable. You discover that it was not a one-time event but that this person led a double life. He was caught in adultery, visited sex workers, or was addicted to pornography, drugs, or alcohol for a long time. Or she was caught with her hands in the till or defrauded others.

Nobody knew. It was a secret for a long time. This person led a double life. Unexpectedly, everything comes out into the open. It's deeply disappointing and upsetting. This happens in our families and in the church, even to the leaders of the church and their wives.

At times like that, we throw up our hands and cry out to God because of the hurt, anger, and mixed emotions: How is it possible? What made this person do these things? How could we have been so wrong about someone we thought we knew?

We wonder, what makes certain people do what they do? Why are they willing to destroy their ministry, the lives of their families, and their reputation in the church and throw it all away? What is it that lures them to destruction?

It's a question that every one of us must face. When something like this happens, we are forced to look at ourselves and ask, "Could I do something like that? Or my husband, my wife, one of my children, or my minister?"

Well, says Paul in 1 Corinthians 10:13, "No temptation has overtaken you that is not common to man." In other words, God says that you and I could be tempted to commit the same horrible sins as others.

That is quite an indictment. Is that really true? Are we that depraved? To answer that question, we must look at how the tempter does his work. How does the devil tempt human beings to sin? We will see that he does that in three ways: first, in how he tempts us; second, in how he deceives us; and finally, we will see how we should respond.

The Temptation

In his 1988 book *Best Sermons*, Haddon W. Robinson provides an extended reflection on Genesis 3 as a case study in temptation. Following his framework, Genesis 3 introduces us to one of God's creatures, the serpent. As one of God's creatures, he is, as God says about all creation, "good." At this point, sin had not yet entered the world. And so, as such, the serpent was not yet an evil creature. He did not have any wicked qualities either.

The fact that he is called crafty (shrewd or cunning, as other translations have it) does not mean that he is devious in an evil sense. No, the word translated as "crafty" refers to quickness of sight, swiftness of motion, and the ability to cleverly adapt to every situation. God endowed the serpent with the ability to be flexible and innovative.

In fact, he was a delightful creature.

But those exceptional qualities of the serpent could be used by an evil, superior intelligence for its own purposes. That is where the devil comes in. He uses the serpent to advance his own evil agenda and speaks and acts through him.

That is always the way the devil works. He uses something beautiful and delightful in God's creation as bait to draw us away from God. That's what he did with the serpent.

Let's see how he does that with Eve. But first, let us keep in mind that Eve was also one of God's good creatures. He created her without sin. At this point, she does not have poisoned blood in her veins like we, born and conceived in sin, do. There is nothing in creation that troubles Eve. She had the perfect start in life. Nothing is lacking in her life, and nothing to spoil her happiness.

For example, she doesn't know what it is to be lonely, or to be full of despair, or to experience rejection or abuse, or famine or disease or hunger. There is no temptation for her to be unfaithful to her husband either. She has the perfect husband. She lives in a beautiful garden. Her life is complete.

That's not the way it is for us, is it? When we sin, we can point to the poor example of others and how we were brought up. Or we can blame our miserable circumstances.

Not Eve. She lives in a pristine environment.

When Jesus Christ was tempted in the wilderness, that was also different for him. He was tempted in a hostile environment. His life was in constant danger. The devil and the world were out to destroy him. He suffered physically. And so he also got hungry, and therefore, the temptation for him to sin was much greater.

But now the devil comes to Eve in that unspoiled state. Pay careful attention to how he goes about his dirty business. If he can tempt *her*, he certainly can tempt you and me. He used the same methods that he still uses. His *modus operandi* has never changed.

In the first place, he disguises himself. He uses one of God's delightful creatures to do that. In the Garden of Eden, he does not warn Eve of his presence, rattling with his tail like a rattlesnake or hissing like a coiled snake ready to strike. He does not come with the roar of a lion either. There is nothing to suggest that there is danger ahead. No, he slides into your life like a trusted companion. He comes, as it says in 2 Corinthians 11:14, like an angel of light.

And please note that he speaks to the woman rather than the man. Why? Well, he knows that Adam was given the command not to eat of the forbidden tree before Eve was even created. As we read in Genesis 2:15–17, God gave him the task to defend and guard the garden. He had to work it, and to keep it, to take care of it. God did not give that command to Eve. She was not even alive at that time.

To be sure, God gave Eve to Adam as his helper, and together they had to carry out God's plan for creation. Together they had dominion. But her task was distinctly different. She is to be the mother of all living.

And now the devil bypasses Adam, who is the authority figure of the garden, and he goes to the one person who, in all of creation, has the most influence over him.

How often does that happen? Rather than going to the head, to the source, people with wicked, self-serving intent go behind their backs and look for the weakest link. Children who are intent on getting their way are very good at that, too, aren't they? They know which parent to pick. And so does anybody who has a tenacious, self-serving agenda. They know with whom they will succeed most in achieving their self-centred goal.

How else does the devil do his dirty work? Well, he gets us focused on one single issue and elevates it to something special to be desired. As something, like they will tell you in a TV commercial, you can't do without. The allure of sin is that it appeals to our greed and our self-centred desires.

And so Satan has her concentrate on one piece of fruit. We don't know what kind of fruit that was. Many people think that it was an apple. But there is no mention of an apple here. It may well have been a cluster of grapes because that is the one fruit most often mentioned in the Bible. But, the fruit as such is not important.

What is striking here is that despite all the many delectable fruits available in the garden, he has her think about that *one* forbidden fruit.

She doesn't need it. She doesn't lack anything. There is no logical reason for her to desire anything else. Until the devil had her think about that one forbidden fruit, she had not given it much thought.

But the devil plants the desire for that one particular fruit in her heart by asking her a question about the forbidden tree in the garden out of the blue. He does not preface his words by saying anything to her about how wonderful it is that God has given her such bounty, that he has given her the freedom to enjoy all of the other trees in the garden. He does not come with anything positive. He never does.

No, he focuses on the negative, on the one *forbidden* fruit.

Isn't that how sin enters our lives? We turn our backs on all the good things and the many blessings God has bestowed upon us and throw it all away for a single sin in our lives. That is what we focus on. That's what we want. Everything else becomes peripheral, unimportant.

Do you know how this happens? Well, this happens when we don't live thankful lives. When, for example, we are not satisfied with the marriage partner God has given us. Or when we are not satisfied with our possessions or with our job. We are jealous of others: "I wish I had what my neighbour has. My life could be much better if I had what he has."

That's the state of mind we come to when we no longer see God's goodness. At that point, we only see what we don't have. And once our focus is shifted, we will do anything to get what we find lacking. If we don't put a stop to it, it will become an obsession.

That's how the first sin started. The devil has Eve focus on what she does not have. And she fell for his deception. She becomes obsessed with that one fruit.

Observe how cleverly he draws her in. As is clear from the way she answered, he does that by the very question he asks. Listen carefully. Satan asked, "Did God actually say, 'You shall not eat of any tree in the garden'?" She answers him that God indeed had said that you shall not eat of the fruit of the tree and that neither shall you touch it, lest you die.

Is that what God said? No. What did he say in Genesis 2:16? He said to the man that he may *surely*, or as other translations have it, that he may *freely* eat of every tree in the garden. She leaves that little word out. He is free to do whatever he wants with every tree in the garden, except this one.

But what does Eve do? She concentrates, not on the freedom, but on the restriction, on the negative.

What else? Did God also say that Adam and Eve were not even allowed to touch the tree? No, God did not say anything about that. Why, then, does the serpent add that? Well, to make God seem more restrictive and severe in his demands than he is. He twists God's Word as a prelude to her sinful behaviour. She fell for the clever language of the devil and listened to him and not to God.

The devil now has her where he wants her. She has taken the bait and is ready to swallow it all, hook, line, and sinker. The temptation is in full swing. Watch him at work.

The Deception

First, he disguises his purposes. He does not whisper in her ear that he is there to tempt her. He does not come baring his teeth and making a show of it.

No, he pretends that he just wants to have a theological discussion with her. He wants her to think that he only wants to make sure that she understands God correctly. In so doing, Satan is trying to make God look restrictive and unkind. He pretends that all he wants from her is some clarification: "Do you think that God really meant what he said? Did you interpret that correctly? Do you think he would deny you the pleasure of that one tree? That doesn't sound like him, does it? He is the God of love, isn't he? And he wants you to enjoy his whole creation, doesn't he?"

That's also how he tempted Jesus in the wilderness: "Do you really think that God the Father wants you to go hungry? Of course not. Why don't you command these stones to become loaves of bread? You can do it. There's nothing to stop you."

That's how he works today as well. The devil whispers in your ear, "Do you think that it is such a big deal that occasionally you

40

stretch the truth in your business dealings so that you can seal the deal? After all, you've got to make a decent living. God doesn't want you to be lacking anything, does he? Go ahead. God will understand."

Or, "What's wrong with a bit of sex outside of marriage? It feels so good. Does God really want to deny you that pleasure? Did he not give us the beautiful gift of sex to enjoy? You are allowed to enjoy life to the fullest."

Or, "It's not such a great sin either, is it, to click on that seductive image in front of you on the computer screen or your device? You're not actually cheating on your partner when you do that. You're just looking. What's the big deal?" And so it goes.

You know what all that leads to, don't you? You will want more. It's never enough. It leads to what we see today, where everybody is out to be true to him or herself. "Just follow your heart. Live a little. Think about yourself first. Satisfy your own desires. You only live once. Be free." That is what the world will tell you, including modern-day psychologists and psychiatrists.

But what happens? Such behaviour becomes habitual. In the end, you become enslaved to that sin. The devil now has you where he wants you. He has you focused on the sinful flesh and how to satisfy your desires. And little by little, you die inside.

Your life becomes empty.

Consider what God says in James 1:14–15, "But each person is tempted when he is lured and enticed by his own desire. Then desire when it has conceived gives birth to sin, and sin when it is fully grown brings forth death."

Death. The devil knows all about that too. Or at least he claims to. That's another way in which he fools and tempts us. He attacks God's Word. Oh sure, he is very subtle and nuanced about it. But listen to what he says to Eve. After Eve tells the serpent that God said they would die if they ate from the tree, he tells her, "You will not surely die."

He is right, but only half right. And that's what makes it a lie. For what does he do? He twists God's Word so that it takes on a different meaning.

He also did that with the Lord Jesus. When he tells Jesus to throw himself down from the highest point of the temple, he quotes Psalm 91:11, namely that God will command his angels concerning him. But he leaves out a little phrase: "to guard you in all your ways." So the complete sentence is "He will command his angels concerning you *to guard you in all your ways.*"

The devil takes verse 11 out of context. For this Psalm is addressed to the one who "dwells in the shelter of the Most High" (vs, 1) and "who trusts in the LORD" (vs. 2). The devil wants Jesus to think that whatever way he chooses is God's way and that God will protect him no matter what he does. The truth is that he only saves those who believe in him and who are righteous through faith. God wants the believer to seek his ways. Therefore, Jesus says to him, "You shall not put the Lord your God to the test." We may never take God's Word out of context to make it mean something that suits us. That's the devil's game. Yet, because of sin, we are all prone to do that. Let's be careful with God's Word within its immediate context and within the context of the whole Bible. That requires diligence and a humble heart.

The devil is also dishonest with Eve about what God says about death. How? We all know what physical death is. You die when your heart is no longer beating, your total brain is no longer functioning, and you are no longer breathing. In that sense, the devil was right. When Eve and Adam took a bite from the fruit, they didn't drop dead. They were still physically alive.

But what does the Bible say about death? On a much deeper level, death is to be abandoned by God and all others. No one cares about you. In God's presence, however, you experience a true and blissful life, together with all of God's children.

In that sense, Adam and Eve died on the day they ate of the forbidden tree. After that, they were no longer allowed to walk and talk with God. They could no longer enjoy God's favour and eat of the tree of life. God banished them from the Garden of Eden.

That is how it is for everyone who sins, which applies to all of us. Because of our sins, we are dead to God. We have walked away from him, and without him, we have no life.

That's why it is so wonderful that he gave his Son to defeat the devil; that in spite of it all, we can share in the victory over sin and evil.

But we can only share in that victory if we confess our sins and repent, not just once but on a regular basis. If not—if we do not fight against our sins—then we will be dead to God in the end. If we do not repent, God will abandon us forever.

That's a horrible prospect.

The devil does not say anything about that, does he? That is because he is not interested in the truth. His only interest is in taking us away from God, from his love and care.

To accomplish that, he attacks not only God's Word, but also his character. He intimates that God has ulterior motives. He says to Eve, "God does not want you to be like him, and for that reason alone, he does not want you to eat of the tree. And what's more, he wants to keep everything for himself. He does not want to share his knowledge and his power. God wants to keep you down. He wants to forbid you the excitement that life offers in its fullness. He doesn't want you to be like him, knowing good and evil, because once you know all that, you will enjoy experiences beyond your wildest dreams. God has an ulterior motive, a hidden agenda, and it's an evil one."

Once the well is poisoned, all the water is polluted. It's one of the most wicked tricks of the devil. He uses this same trick all the time, also today. Shrewd politicians are very good at it. When they can't defeat their political opponents' ideas and success, then they will attack their character.

Once you go down that road, you doubt God's goodness. The next thing you will do is doubt God's Word. If you do not believe that God is there for you always and that he cares about you, then the work of the tempter is complete. You have placed yourself outside of God and his kingdom.

But the devil wants to keep that eventuality hidden from you. He never tells you the truth. He keeps you in the dark about the consequences of disobedience against God.

If anybody knows about the consequence, it is the devil, for he was thrown out of heaven because of his disobedience. His fate is sealed. As it says in Revelation 20:10, he will be thrown into the Lake of Fire, where he will be tormented day and night forever and ever. He knows it. And the devil wants us to share his fate. Be watchful.

The Response

And so, how do we protect ourselves? How do we respond? Well, note how Jesus defeats the devil. What does he do? He used the power of the Word of God. He quotes the Bible. He says, "It is written." Very simple. Yet quite profound.

If you want to protect yourself from evil, go to God's Word—all of it. Don't take it out of context, as the devil does. Be faithful to the Word. Let God speak to you, not your sinful flesh, not your own desires so that you twist God's Word to suit you.

That takes self-awareness and knowledge. You must know what you believe and why. But don't think that when the Bible speaks about knowledge, that means that you should be able to quote Scripture frontwards and backwards. That's good, of course, but ultimately, it means having intimate knowledge of God and his ways. It is the kind of knowledge you have about your loving father and mother and your wife or your husband to whom you have long been married. You have gone through many things together and learned to trust and depend on each other. You know how your partner is going to react in certain situations.

That's the kind of knowledge you must have about God, our perfect covenant partner, who always reacts in the right way, with compassion, understanding, and patience. To know God means to know what it is to live close to him and to love him.

Every day you call upon him. You talk to him. You pour out your heart to him when you are in trouble. You give him thanks for the many things with which he provides you. And you want to please him because you know he loves you. To know him means to trust him. To depend on him for everything. To trust his character, his goodness, and his love for you.

When God created Adam and Eve, he made a covenant with them. He made promises. He gave man and woman the highest place in all of creation. He gave them a place of honour. He gave them the ability to be in a relationship with him and with each other.

The fall into sin ultimately did not change that. He still loves you and still wants you to be in a relationship with him. Even

45

though you fall into sin, even into some horrible sin, and even if you live in it for a while, he still deeply cares for you. He will keep on beckoning you to come back.

Of course, the time must also come when you want to go back to him. You are miserable without him and want to be in his presence again. And then you humble yourself before him. Once again, you acknowledge that he is the God of love and that he does not want to deny you any good thing. God wants you to be near him. He does not want to leave you in your sins.

For that reason, you have to listen to him and not to the devil. James says in chapter 4:7, "Resist the devil, and he will flee from you."

Yet, how often do we not fall for the devil's tricks? I know I do. Every day, in one way or the other, he has us do things against God's Word. That is why we need to ask for the forgiveness of sins every day. We need God to restore us and to renew us. That is an ongoing activity.

We need God's help to survive. Listen to what God says in Hebrews 2:16–18:

> For surely it is not angels he helps, but Abraham's descendants. For this reason he had to be made like his brothers in every way, in order that he might become a merciful and faithful high priest in service to God, and that he might make atonement for the sins of the people. Because he himself suffered when he was tempted, he is able to help those who are being tempted. (NIV84)

On Golgotha, our Lord and Saviour Jesus Christ paid for our sins. He nailed our sins to the cross with him, so that we can stand before God unafraid and full of joy. Even though we are led into temptation time and again, and sin against God and our fellow man, through faith in Christ we are declared innocent.

What great love he has shown us. He was obedient even in the most horrible circumstances. He obeyed his Father in heaven during the most difficult and trying times. He never gave up.

You may not give up, either. If some sin has you in its grip, run for help, to Jesus. Repent. He will help you and forgive you and love you.

The devil cannot claim us. As long as you go to God time and again, for forgiveness, for renewal, for strength and wisdom, for the gift of life, he will grant it to you. He will grant you eternal life.

And so: Don't listen to the devil. Listen to God.

Always.

Reflection

1. In Matthew 4:1–11, we learn about the temptation of Jesus. How did Jesus withstand each temptation—from hunger, power, and wealth? What can you learn from each of the responses of Jesus in terms of abandoning the things of this world?

2. The devil tricked Adam and Eve into concentrating on one forbidden piece of fruit, making them forget about all the other good fruit they were allowed to eat. What destructive "fruit" in your life makes you lose sight of all the good things in your life? After identifying how you lose sight of what is good, reflect on the ways you may be regenerated by the Spirit of God.

Chapter 3
Circumcision as a Sign of The Covenant

"For we are the circumcision,
who worship by the Spirit of God
and glory in Christ Jesus
and put no confidence in the flesh."
Philippians 3:3

"In him also you were circumcised
with a circumcision made without hands,
by putting off the body of the flesh,
by the circumcision of Christ,
having been buried with him in baptism,
in which you were also raised with him through faith in
the powerful working of God,
who raised him from the dead."
Colossians 2:11–12

Introduction

The fall into sin had momentous consequences for all of creation, especially for humanity. Everything became broken and subject to death and decay. The Lord God did not want this situation to be permanent, which is why he made a promise to Adam and Eve and their offspring that through the seed of the woman, he would crush the head of the serpent (Genesis 3:15). In other words,

Satan will be destroyed, and sin and the effects of sin will be done away with forever.

But how would that happen? And when? It would be a long time before that promise would be fulfilled. How does God's promise continue to function in the minds and hearts of God's people? That's very difficult in a world full of broken promises. Too often, we human beings treat our promises as if they are merely suggestions. Ever since the fall into sin, we are no longer reliable and often say one thing, yet do another. The adage "Promises are made to be broken" rings true.

There are many reasons for that. External factors such as health issues, financial difficulties, or unexpected events often interfere with our ability to keep our promises. To manipulate or deceive others for personal gain, we knowingly make promises but have no intention of keeping them. And sometimes, because of a busy schedule or distractions, we genuinely forget about our promises.

God, however, wants to assure his people that he always keeps his promises, is reliable, and never goes back on his word. Thus, he made a covenant with us, a binding agreement between God and his people, involving a relationship with unfailing commitments and strong bonds.

The Lord God himself made this covenant with man. He initiated it and wants his children to live according to it. Thus, God did not just give the covenant to them, but he created them as covenant creatures. It is a living relationship where two parties, God and his people, constantly interact. Whereas God is the perfect covenant partner, man is not. He is sinful and, because of that, breaks the covenant with God all the time. Through the mercy of Jesus Christ, God maintains the relationship into eternity. And so we must show our thanks to him for his mercy and do our utmost to keep the laws of God.

God does not want us to doubt that he is always faithful to his Word. We need assurances and reminders of God's truthfulness and reliability. That is why he gave the sign and seal of his covenant, which in the Old Testament is circumcision. In this chapter, we will see the incredible significance of the covenant of circumcision.

Scripture

Genesis 15:1–21

God's Covenant with Abram

1 After these things the word of the LORD came to Abram in a vision: "Fear not, Abram, I am your shield; your reward shall be very great."

2 But Abram said, "O Lord God, what will you give me, for I continue childless, and the heir of my house is Eliezer of Damascus?"

3 And Abram said, "Behold, you have given me no offspring, and a member of my household will be my heir."

4 And behold, the word of the LORD came to him: "This man shall not be your heir; your very own son shall be your heir."

5 And he brought him outside and said, "Look toward heaven, and number the stars, if you are able to number them." Then he said to him, "So shall your offspring be."

6 And he believed the LORD, and he counted it to him as righteousness.

7 And he said to him, "I am the LORD who brought you out from Ur of the Chaldeans to give you this land to possess."

8 But he said, "O Lord God, how am I to know that I shall possess it?"

9 He said to him, "Bring me a heifer three years old, a female goat three years old, a ram three years old, a turtledove, and a young pigeon."

10 And he brought him all these, cut them in half, and laid each half over against the other. But he did not cut the birds in half.

11 And when birds of prey came down on the carcasses, Abram drove them away.

12 As the sun was going down, a deep sleep fell on Abram. And behold, dreadful and great darkness fell upon him.

13 Then the LORD said to Abram, "Know for certain that your offspring will be sojourners in a land that is not theirs and will be servants there, and they will be afflicted for four hundred years.

14 But I will bring judgment on the nation that they serve, and afterward they shall come out with great possessions.

15 As for you, you shall go to your fathers in peace; you shall be buried in a good old age.

16 And they shall come back here in the fourth generation, for the iniquity of the Amorites is not yet complete."

17 When the sun had gone down and it was dark, behold, a smoking fire pot and a flaming torch passed between these pieces.

18 On that day the LORD made a covenant with Abram, saying, "To your offspring I give this land, from the river of Egypt to the great river, the river Euphrates,

19 the land of the Kenites, the Kenizzites, the Kadmonites,

20 the Hittites, the Perizzites, the Rephaim,

21 the Amorites, the Canaanites, the Girgashites and the Jebusites."

Genesis 17:1–14

1 When Abram was ninety-nine years old the Lord appeared to Abram and said to him, "I am God Almighty; walk before me, and be blameless,

2 that I may make my covenant between me and you, and may multiply you greatly."

3 Then Abram fell on his face. And God said to him,

4 "Behold, my covenant is with you, and you shall be the father of a multitude of nations.

5 No longer shall your name be called Abram, but your name shall be Abraham, for I have made you the father of a multitude of nations.

6 I will make you exceedingly fruitful, and I will make you into nations, and kings shall come from you.

7 And I will establish my covenant between me and you and your offspring after you throughout their generations for an everlasting covenant, to be God to you and to your offspring after you.

8 And I will give to you and to your offspring after you the land of your sojournings, all the land of Canaan, for an everlasting possession, and I will be their God."

9 And God said to Abraham, "As for you, you shall keep my covenant, you and your offspring after you throughout their generations.

10 This is my covenant, which you shall keep, between me and you and your offspring after you: Every male among you shall be circumcised.

11 You shall be circumcised in the flesh of your foreskins, and it shall be a sign of the covenant between me and you.

12 He who is eight days old among you shall be circumcised. Every male throughout your generations, whether born in your house or bought with your money from any foreigner who is not of your offspring,

13 both he who is born in your house and he who is bought with your money, shall surely be circumcised. So shall my covenant be in your flesh an everlasting covenant.

14 Any uncircumcised male who is not circumcised in the flesh of his foreskin shall be cut off from his people; he has broken my covenant."

Circumcision as a Sign of the Covenant

Abraham is known as the father of all believers (Romans 4:11). During his entire life, the Lord God wanted Abraham to depend on God alone and to trust him. Abraham had to depend on him when he told him to leave his country and his family and go where he would show him. He had to trust in God and believe him when God told him he would make him the father of many nations.

In Genesis 15, we read that the Lord God took Abraham outside and told him that he would make Abraham's offspring as numerous as the stars in the sky, and Abraham believed. The Lord credited Abraham's faith to him as righteousness.

The events of Genesis 17 took place some twenty-three years later. Abraham is ninety-nine years old. He still does not have an heir. He and Sarah are childless. Nevertheless, Abraham must continue to believe the promise of the Lord that he will give him children through his wife Sarah and that God will make Abraham a great nation.

Continuing to believe is hard, especially if you don't see any evidence that God will fulfil his promises. Abraham needed reassurance, especially now that, humanly speaking, it was impossible for him and Sarah to have a child. They are too old. Nobody has children at their age.

And so, in Genesis 17, the Lord speaks to Abraham again. The Lord knows that Abraham needs to hear from him again to assure him. Abraham needs to be strengthened in his faith. Therefore,

God must tell Abraham once again about his covenant ways and how he alone is the One who gives life. He is the God of miracles. Everything is possible with him. His word is the word of truth and he is always faithful to his promises.

Abraham must know that when God speaks and makes promises, he will fulfil them. But he will do that in his way and in his own time. That's hard for us mortals to deal with and understand. It's hard for us to wait.

Therefore, in Genesis 17, the Lord gives Abraham the rite of circumcision as a sign of his covenant promises. Abraham needs a signpost, something physical that he can cling to, something that keeps reminding him of the certainty of God's promises. We all need that, don't we?

In Genesis 15, just after Abraham defeated Chedorlaomer and the kings who were with him, the Lord seals his covenant by going through the blood of the animals cut in two. This solemn ritual, which in the day was known as "cutting a covenant," involved the death of animals and the binding of people to a promise. This was done as a declaration that, if they failed to keep their word, they deserved the same fate as the animals. In this way, the Lord initially confirmed his covenant with Abraham.

But in Genesis 17, the Lord adds another element to the covenant. He now adds the sign of circumcision. The act of circumcision as such was not new to Abraham. It was already known to the people of the ancient Near East of Abraham's day. Virtually all the nations around them practiced circumcision.

Only the Mesopotamians, from which Abraham himself came, and the Canaanites in the land of Palestine, among whom Abraham now lived, did not practice this rite. But no doubt they were familiar with the custom, for they were aware of each other's practices through the contacts they had with each other.

And so, the Lord didn't need to tell Abraham how to perform the circumcision rite. Abraham could find that out easily enough from the foreign servants in his household. Among his servants were also Egyptians, who widely practiced the rite of circumcision.

Yet, the Lord does add a new element to the practice. What God does is he ties circumcision to his covenant promises and demands.

As we know from ancient sources, in the ancient Near East, circumcision had a completely different purpose. With those who lived there, the practice was closely tied to marriage. It was done to prepare a young man for marriage. He was circumcised to remove any possible hindrance to intercourse and thereby prevent any impediment to bringing forth offspring.

In ancient Egypt, it was usually the task of the future father-in-law to perform the rite. The father of the bride or another elder would often oversee the circumcision as a way to ensure that the groom was fit to marry their daughter. They believed that, with the removal of the foreskin, an obstacle to the creation of life was removed.

But now, look at how God uses that concept to clarify his covenant with Abraham. For what does he do? First, he commands that all the males in Abraham's household be circumcised, not as a preparation for marriage but as a preparation for the Lord.

Therefore, the Lord does not want the males to be circumcised at the time just before their marriage but already at the tender age of eight days. He wants all the males to be circumcised when they are barely out of the womb. In this way, the Lord shows that he is the Creator of life and that if there are any obstacles to life, he is the One to remove those obstacles. The openings and passages to life are totally in his hands.

This is an essential message for Abraham at this time of uncertainty, for the Lord had given Abraham the promise of new life. He had promised him a son. Indeed, he had promised him more than a son. He had promised to make him the father of many nations. Yet, at this point, Abraham was still without offspring.

To be sure, Abraham already had Ishmael as his son through his concubine, Hagar, but the ultimate blessing of the Lord would not come through Ishmael but through a son brought into the world through Abraham and Sarah. The Lord would fulfill that promise, even though they were at an advanced age.

Now, we also come to a deeper understanding of circumcision. Abraham is blessed, not so much because of his physical offspring, but because of his spiritual offspring, that is, all those who believe. Through Abraham, the seed of the woman, as announced in Paradise after the fall into sin, would continue. Ultimately, the seed of the woman would culminate in the birth of Christ. He is the Head of the church, which is the gathering of true believers.

And so, the church does not grow and increase through the opening of the womb in the first place but through the opening of God's Word. God comes to us with his word of promise. He says to us, as he does to Abraham, that he is our Father and that we are his children through the adoption as sons. He comes to us with the promise of eternal life. The promise comes through God alone. Our lives are not in our own hands. Only he can give physical life so that children can be born to God's covenant people to have a special relationship with God through faith.

Whereas unbelievers thought that a physical obstacle to life is removed through circumcision, God shows in circumcision that life is in his hands and that only he can remove any obstacle to life. Life is not in the hands of man; it is in the hands of God. For that reason, he makes circumcision a sign of the covenant.

He also gives us the wonderful news that his covenant is everlasting. That means that our lives continue beyond the grave. For in the life hereafter, we will dwell with God forever. This is only possible if the obstacle of sin is removed.

Removal of Sin

And now we come to an even deeper understanding of circumcision, to the true meaning and the most significant part of circumcision as a sign and the seal of the covenant. Circumcision has to do with the removal of sin. It points to the restoration of life with God.

Isn't that also what he promised? He repeatedly promised to remove the obstacle of sin through the shedding of blood. That is why God instituted the sacrifices in the temple. The blood in the tabernacle and the temple flowed continually. And you know what the shed blood points to, don't you? It points to the blood of Christ.

With circumcision, the foreskin of the male reproductive organ would be removed and thrown away. Why? Well, the removal of the foreskin symbolizes the removal of sin. In this way, circumcision looks forward to the coming of Christ, who would remove sin from the world through his shed blood. For what is the obstacle to eternal life? Sin. Sin is the obstacle to true life. If our sins were not removed through Christ's blood, humankind could never be saved and live with God.

For that reason, blood also takes on such a deep significance in the Scriptures. In the Old Testament, the animals' blood had to be shed in a sacrifice acceptable to God. Blood would have to be shed to point to the removal of sin. That blood pointed to the blood to be shed by the Saviour of the world, by Christ. He had to shed his blood before the obstacle of man's sin could be removed.

As we read in Hebrews 9:18, "Therefore not even the first covenant was inaugurated without blood." That shedding of blood looked forward to the sacrifice of Christ on the cross. In the circumcision act, blood had to be shed first as well.

After Christ, blood no longer had to be shed. And so circumcision was now no longer a sign of the covenant. As we will see in the next chapter, baptism took its place. Circumcision looked forward to Christ, but baptism looks back at Christ to what he had done. Baptism points to the cleansing through the blood of Christ and the great event on Golgotha. So now also, baptism is a sign of the covenant.

A male child was to be circumcised on the eighth day. During the Sinaitic legislation, a woman was unclean until seven days after she had given birth. On the eighth day, she would be considered clean. On the eighth day, a child would no longer be rendered unclean by his mother touching him.

That illustrates yet another point. In reality, a child was unclean from the first day of his birth and also after the seventh day. That is why David exclaimed in Psalm 51:5, "Behold, I was brought forth in iniquity, and in sin did my mother conceive me." We are polluted by sin all the days of our earthly lives. Ultimately, only God could remove the stain of sin.

That is something you must believe because, in this way, you give the honour and glory to him. We are nothing without him. Our sins need to be removed through the blood of Christ. And that is why we have to bring our children up with that covenant knowledge. As children grow up, they also have to learn to accept that act of cleansing through faith. We and our children must believe that only God gives the openings to life.

Already in the circumcision act, the ritual cleansing through the Lord Jesus Christ is present. Ultimately, the same applies to baptism as to circumcision. What we see is that the covenant has its continuation through faith. God first comes to man with his promises. This is also what he did with Abraham. He comes with his promises first. But then he also comes with the demand of covenant. Abraham must accept this covenant in faith. He has to listen to God's Word. He has to open his heart and mind to him.

In this way, we also see the symbolic significance of circumcision when the Lord tells his people Israel in Deuteronomy 10:16 that they must circumcise the foreskin of their hearts, and elsewhere that they must circumcise their ears and speak with circumcised lips. He warns them that their hearts, ears, and lips are not to be plugged up with sin lest they be closed to the God of life.

Someone whose ears are plugged up because of sin and whose heart is closed to the Lord cannot receive the gift of life from the Lord. God's people must listen to the Lord our God. We must open up our hearts to him so that he can enter. That is possible only if we repent from our sins.

The Extent of the Covenant

Genesis 17:12 tells us that every male child had to be circumcised, including all those bought with money from a foreigner. Here, we also see the extent of the covenant. Abraham was the head of a very large household. He had many slaves who were under his authority. He was responsible for them as a father is responsible for his own children.

By extending his covenant to his whole household, we see God's great mercy. He uses Abraham to be a blessing to all those who are under his roof. He makes his covenant with all of them.

In this way, the Lord again shows that the covenant does not depend on the flesh but on the good pleasure of the Lord alone. He uses Abraham to extend his covenant to Abraham's whole household. As outlined in the next chapters, God's covenant extends to families and their households. God knows what significant and powerful influences happen within family units. Children are in the covenant by God's choice and for their benefit.

But by giving the promise to all those who were under Abraham's influence, he also shows the tremendous responsibility Abraham has. Abraham is to bring them up in the way of the Lord. He is to be an example to them. He is to show them and teach them how to walk with God in faith. God's promises never change. But when the Lord God comes to man with his promise, man must also accept that promise in faith. You break with the covenant if you do not accept it in faith.

This we see happen later on with Ishmael. He had to be circumcised along with the rest of them. But later, he ridicules Isaac. He laughs at him (Genesis 21:9). He does not want to accept that the Lord determines how we will be saved and by whom we will be saved. So, ultimately, Ishmael denied that the Christ, the Anointed One from the Lord, would be born through Isaac and not through him. Ishmael, too, could have been saved through the covenant. But he did not want to accept God's promise of true life through faith in God. He did not acknowledge that only through Isaac could he be part of the covenant.

Abraham is told that only the males should receive the sign of the covenant. Does that mean then that the women were not included? No, that is certainly not the case. God considered it sufficient that the promise of the covenant be extended to the woman through the man. This had to do with the special position the woman held in the Old Testament.

It is not that the woman in the Old Testament had an inferior position to the man. A woman is equal to a man, even in the Old Testament. As mentioned above, God's covenant is with families. That includes girls. That is made all the more clear in the New Testament wherein girls are also to be baptized. But the woman's position is different. She has a different role in the history of redemption—a vital role. She is blessed through the bearing of children (1 Timothy 2:15).

Ultimately, she would be included through Christ. For through Christ, the promise of eternal life extends to her as well as to man.

The Fulfilment of the Covenant

After the death of Christ, circumcision as a sign of the covenant was abolished. There was no longer any need to shed blood. Christ's blood was sufficient for all. The blood of circumcision points to the blood of Jesus Christ, but once that was shed once for all, there was no more need.

Furthermore, Christ removed any obstacle that prevented humankind from being adopted as children. He removed the obstacle of sin. He opened the way to life, to true life in him.

We might say that Christ's whole work of redemption was circumcision work. Indeed, that is also how the Scriptures refer to it. Christ's death is the covenant circumcision which has set us apart for eternity to God. The cross took away the foreskin of our sin. That is why we read about salvation in circumcision terms. Paul writes, "For no one is a Jew who is merely one outwardly, nor is circumcision outward and physical. But a Jew is one inwardly, and circumcision is a matter of the heart, by the Spirit, not by the letter. His praise is not from man but from God" (Romans 2:28–29).

Colossians 2:11 tells us this about the New Testament

believers: "In him also you were circumcised with a circumcision made without hands, by putting off the body of the flesh, by the circumcision of Christ." And in Philippians 3:3, we read, "For we are the circumcision, who worship by the Spirit of God and glory in Christ Jesus and put no confidence in the flesh."

Christ himself was also physically circumcised when he was eight days old. That was so because he took on the sins of all humankind. Christ was circumcised to demonstrate that he took on our sins. He came under the law so that he might fulfill the law. For that reason, Christ was also cut off, circumcised from his people. He was cut off from God when he hung on the cross and cried out, "My God, My God, why have you forsaken me?"

Golgotha was the ultimate covenant circumcision. That is where our Lord and Saviour dealt with sin in a most radical way. By doing away with sin, Christ was totally faithful to the covenant. He fulfilled the demands of the covenant and the promises of the covenant.

And now, through faith, we, too, are part of the covenant. We must believe that Christ died for our sins and washed them away through his blood and Spirit. Faith in Jesus Christ gives us access to the blessing of forgiveness and renewal.

We must put our faith into action. We must not want to have anything to do with sin. Our hearts and ears must not be plugged up with sin and corruption. But they are to be circumcised in Christ. We must believe that Christ has removed all the obstacles to true life.

So, we, as covenant children, must show our thankfulness by submitting to God's covenant law.

Abraham and his household could not just receive the covenant sign either and then sit back and do nothing. No, Abraham had to accept the covenant in faith and put that faith into action. He had to instruct all those who were part of his household in the ways of the covenant.

Receiving the sign of the covenant brings tremendous responsibilities, including for us today. We, too, must instruct our children in the way of the Lord and to have them instructed therein.

However, it's more than that. To teach them properly, we also must be examples of faith. Living examples. Our children must learn from us what it means to trust in the Lord and to walk in his ways. They must see from us that we are not anxious about what tomorrow will bring but that we are at peace knowing that God will provide for us. They must see from their parents that they are satisfied human beings, glad for God's material and spiritual gifts. Not grumblers who are never satisfied and find fault with everyone and everything.

Our children must also see us walking humbly with God in the realization of our sins. Parents must walk humbly before their children. They must walk humbly with others, and when they wrong us, our children must see that we are willing and eager even to forgive. They must witness in their parents how important it is to keep relationships strong, both their relationship with God and their relationship with others.

Children of believing parents must also learn that God's covenant promises and demands also apply to them. You do not leave it up to them to choose whether they should worship the Lord. No, the Lord has already made them his children, and the promises are already given to them. And now they have to learn to live out of those promises. That is also how Isaac and Jacob were brought up.

We must choose. The Scriptures repeatedly tell us that we must choose whom we serve, whether the gods of the world or the God of the Bible. But we choose only because God has chosen us first.

That is why, time and again, we must choose to do his will, not our own. Every moment of every day we must choose not to want to sin. That's what it means to be a covenant child. It means that we speak with circumcised lips and have circumcised hearts and ears. It means that we walk close to God and listen to what he says to us in his Word.

In this way, we can also be sure that we and our house will receive the blessing of the covenant. We can be confident that Christ's act of circumcision is also our act of circumcision.

Through the blood of Christ, our sins have been removed. The way to God, the way to life, has been opened. Such is the blessing of the covenant. Isn't that wonderful? It is the most excellent gift anyone could ever receive.

Reflection

1. The Lord God promises the forgiveness of sins and eternal life to all those who believe in him. How important are those promises to you? How do these promises reveal themselves in your relationship with God and others?

2. Circumcision points to the need for the sacrifice of Jesus Christ to shed his blood for us. According to Philippians 2:7, he emptied himself of all the glory and majesty he had as the Son of God. It was a tremendous sacrifice. To believe in the forgiveness of sins means that we must also forgive others. What kinds of sacrifices does God expect from us? Are you willing to make those

sacrifices? Can you give examples of sacrifices you have made and are willing to make?

Chapter 4
Infant Baptism

"Jesus said,
'Let the little children come to me
and do not hinder them,
for to such belongs
the kingdom of heaven.'"

Matthew 19:14

"Baptism is not only a sacrament
of our union with Christ;
it is also a sacrament
of our communion as saints."

John Calvin

Introduction

The Christian practice of baptism is not without controversy. Some Christian denominations, like Baptists and many Evangelical churches, practice "believers' baptism" or "credobaptism." They emphasize the symbolism of baptism as an outward expression of a person's personal faith and repentance. Since infants cannot make a conscious decision to believe and repent, these churches argue that only individuals who have personally accepted Jesus

Christ should be baptized.

Many other churches practice infant baptism, such as the Roman Catholic Church, the Eastern Orthodox Church, and some Protestant denominations like Anglicans, Lutherans, and Reformed churches. According to their perspective, baptism is seen as a sign of the covenant between God and believers, like circumcision in the Old Testament, as discussed in the previous chapter. Just as Israelite infants were circumcised to signify their inclusion in the covenant community, these churches baptize infants to signify their inclusion into the Christian community.

What is the correct position? The problem for us is that the Bible doesn't state explicitly that children must be baptized. But you do not find the command in the Bible either that children are not allowed to be baptized. Hence, our task involves a diligent examination of the biblical text. By carefully analyzing what the Bible has to say about this matter, we can uncover the truth regarding the baptism of infants.

That is also what we do with other doctrines. The Trinity, for example. Nowhere in the Bible is the word "Trinity" mentioned. Jehovah's Witnesses will make a big deal of that. And yet, we can clearly conclude from the Bible that God exists in three persons: Father, Son, and Holy Spirit. Each person of the Trinity is plainly shown to be God. Therefore, we speak biblically when we speak about God the Father, God the Son, and God the Holy Spirit. A careful reading of the Bible and faithful submission to God's Word does not allow you to come to a different conclusion.

With infant baptism, we must also carefully examine the Bible. In so doing, I believe that we cannot come to any other conclusion than that children of believers belong to God's covenant and ought to be baptized. As we will see in this chapter, that makes sense not only biblically but also historically and psychologically.

Scripture

Romans 2:25–3:4

25 For circumcision indeed is of value if you obey the law, but if you break the law, your circumcision becomes uncircumcision.

26 So, if a man who is uncircumcised keeps the precepts of the law, will not his uncircumcision be regarded as circumcision?

27 Then he who is physically uncircumcised but keeps the law will condemn you who have the written code and circumcision but break the law.

28 For no one is a Jew who is merely one outwardly, nor is circumcision outward and physical.

29 But a Jew is one inwardly, and circumcision is a matter of the heart, by the Spirit, not by the letter. His praise is not from man but from God.

3 Then what advantage has the Jew? Or what is the value of circumcision?

2 Much in every way. To begin with, the Jews were entrusted with the oracles of God.

3 What if some were unfaithful? Does their faithlessness nullify the faithfulness of God?

4 By no means! Let God be true though every one were a liar, as it is written, "That you may be justified in your words, and prevail when you are judged."

1 Corinthians 7:12–16

12 To the rest I say (I, not the Lord) that if any brother has a wife who is an unbeliever, and she consents to live with him, he should not divorce her.

13 If any woman has a husband who is an unbeliever, and he consents to live with her, she should not divorce him.

14 For the unbelieving husband is made holy because of his wife, and the unbelieving wife is made holy because of her husband. Otherwise your children would be unclean, but as it is, they are holy.

15 But if the unbelieving partner separates, let it be so. In such cases the brother or sister is not enslaved. God has called you to peace.

16 For how do you know, wife, whether you will save your husband? Or how do you know, husband, whether you will save your wife?

Heidelberg Catechism

74. Q. Should infants, too, be baptized?

A. Yes.
Infants as well as adults
belong to God's covenant and congregation.[1]

Through Christ's blood
the redemption from sin
and the Holy Spirit, who works faith,
are promised to them
no less than to adults.[2]

Therefore, by baptism, as sign of the covenant,
they must be incorporated into the Christian church
and distinguished from the children of unbelievers.[3]

This was done in the old covenant by circumcision,[4]
in place of which baptism was instituted
in the new covenant.[5]

[1] Gen 17:7; Mt 19:14.
[2] Ps 22:10; Is 44:1–3; Acts 2:38, 39; 16:31.
[3] Acts 10:47; 1 Cor 7:14.
[4] Gen 17:9–14.
[5] Col 2:11–13.

The Role of Faith

The main argument against infant baptism is that when baptism is mentioned in the New Testament, it is always done in connection with faith. Mark 16:16 says that you must believe and be baptized. Baptists will go to great lengths to emphasize that and refer to many Scripture passages to show that when someone expresses his faith in the Lord Jesus Christ, baptism follows.

For example, in Acts 8, we read about the conversion of the Ethiopian eunuch. This man, who was already a believer in God, came from Jerusalem where he worshiped in the temple. Subsequently, upon receiving the gospel message from Philip concerning the Lord Jesus, he embraced this faith. Because of his new faith in the Lord Jesus, he inquired if there was any reason for him not to be baptized. When they came upon some water, they stopped the chariot he was riding in, and immediately he was baptized.

There are many other stories about those who were baptized after they believed. Think about Lydia, who also worshiped God and whose heart was opened to respond to Paul's message of the good news about the Lord Jesus Christ. We read in Acts 16:15 that she was subsequently baptized along with the members of her household.

In Acts 16, we also read about the Philippian jailer who came to faith after Paul preached the gospel to him. We read in verse 33 that subsequently, "He was baptized at once, he and all his family."

There are other examples. Thus, the point is well taken: those who hold to the baptism of believers only are correct that baptism must take place after coming to faith.

But that is *not* the point of difference we have with them. Reformed believers agree that adults must be baptized because of their faith.

What then are the differences? So far, there are none. We all agree. It is true that the baptism of adults is an infrequent event in churches practising infant baptism. In "evangelical churches," it is a much more frequent event. There is a lot of excitement and enthusiasm around this. So, it seems they are more in tune with the New Testament church as described in the Bible.

But let's put that within the context and the times and circumstances in which this was done. We are at the beginning of the New Testament period when there was a significant change from the Old Testament to the New Testament. That is because of Christ, the Lamb who shed his blood for sinners once and for all and who fulfilled all the ceremonial laws.

So, the Lord's Supper came in place of Passover. And, as Reformed people firmly believe, baptism came in place of circumcision. That is why, when baptism was introduced, everyone, including whole households, had to be baptized.

Therefore, you can understand that believers' baptism was frequent at the beginning of the New Testament. Many people came to believe in Jesus and wanted to have the new sign of the covenant. They were baptized in accordance with the command of Jesus to his disciples just before he ascended into heaven: "Go therefore and make disciples of all nations, baptizing them in the name of the Father and of the Son and of the Holy Spirit" (Matthew 28:19). What Mark recorded in Mark 16:16—"Whoever believes and is baptized will be saved"—is parallel to the ending of Matthew and is a mission-minded directive: disciple the nations and baptize. In such a context, adults will need to be baptized, and many were.

But later, when infant baptism had become the norm, the

baptism of adults was no longer as frequent. Circumcision of adults in the Old Testament was also quite rare; then, the circumcision of babies was the norm. There were very few adult circumcisions. Most adults were already circumcised.

But that doesn't mean that adult circumcision didn't happen. It did, for there were proselytes who came to the Jewish faith as adults. To belong to the Jewish community and to be able to worship in the temple, you needed to be circumcised. And so they were.

But that was the exception. Everybody else was already circumcised.

From Old to New

The main argument against those who hold to baptism for adults only is that baptism replaces circumcision. That is not something, of course, that those who hold to adult baptism agree with. They state that circumcision was historically an initiation rite into the ethnic community and that circumcision sets you apart from the other nations, making you only part of God's covenant community, for then you belong to Abraham, and to his offspring, to Israel.

But is that all it does? For what is circumcision? Both sides of the issue will agree that circumcision is the sign of the old covenant, and that baptism is the sign of the new covenant. There is no escaping that. The Bible clearly teaches that.

There is no escaping the fact either that both circumcision and baptism are connected to faith. That connection is quite clear from Romans 3:30, namely that God "will justify the circumcised by faith and the uncircumcised through faith." And so, for adults, faith was also necessary to be circumcised.

But what does circumcision signify? As we saw in the previous chapter, it signifies more than just belonging to Abraham and his seed. It signifies impurity and the consequent need for the shedding of blood and the removal of sin. The piece of foreskin at the time of the circumcision was thrown away, just like our sin has to be done away with.

With Christ, the shedding of blood is no longer necessary. Why not? Because Christ shed his blood once and for all. For that reason, circumcision had to be abolished. Something else had to take its place.

Clearly, this is where baptism comes in. Baptism also signifies doing away with sin. In Colossians 2:11, therefore, Paul calls baptism the circumcision "done without hands." To perform the ritual of circumcision, you had to be skilled with your hands. It is a delicate operation. Therefore, with baptism, such skillful use of the hands was no longer necessary. Baptism is circumcision without hands.

Baptism is Like a Picture

Now the question is, if infants in the Old Testament needed to be circumcised as a sign of the covenant and the removal of sin, why are there those who refuse to baptize children?

There are many reasons for that. At the time of the Reformation, the Anabaptists (as they were called then) came to their position because they wanted to make a radical break with the practices of the Roman Catholic Church. And that's understandable, for, among other things, the Roman Catholics had made baptism more than it is. According to Roman Catholic doctrine, you receive God's sanctifying grace through the water of baptism. God's grace is poured into you as soon as you receive the sacrament. And without God's grace, you cannot be saved and are cleansed from your original sin in Adam. That is why it is so crucial for Roman Catholic parents to have their children baptized as soon as possible. In emergencies, even a nurse can baptize a child.

In this way, no matter what kind of life you lead, as long as you are baptized and as long as you partake of the other sacraments of the church throughout your life, you can still be saved. You may have to spend time in purgatory for a while, but ultimately, you will be saved because of the sacraments you received in the church. In this way, baptism becomes a ticket to heaven. And the connection between faith and baptism is removed.

That is of great concern. Understandably, the Anabaptists no longer wanted anything to do with that. We agree that we may never think that baptism as such saves you. It doesn't. It is merely a sign, a picture representing the real thing.

You may not confuse the picture with the real thing. For example, if you were to see a picture of the king of England, you could say to someone, "That is the king," and then you would not be lying. But, no one would think that you mean that that is actually the king himself in that picture as if he could walk out of the picture. No, that picture only represents him. It shows us what he looks like and reminds us of what he stands for.

The same thing is true of baptism. It is only a picture of what it represents. The water represents the blood of Christ through which we are cleansed. Therefore, the water of baptism as such doesn't save you. No, it points to the blood of the Lord Jesus Christ. Baptism doesn't automatically save you. And that is why when children come of age, they must make a profession of their faith.

If a child does not come to that point and does not want to live as a child of God and belong to God's covenant people, then it is as if they never received the baptism. No doubt, the baptism itself was real and contained all the promises, but when you walk away from it, it is no longer real for you. If those who have been baptized no longer live according to what baptism signifies and do not repent, they will be treated as unbelievers and considered to be covenant breakers.

Today, many people are baptized "heathens." They were baptized as children, but they never really came to faith. And even though they were baptized, they will not be saved unless they repent.

But there were many circumcised "heathens" as well. The Scriptures throughout tell us about them. Numerous Israelites, God's covenant people, rejected him. They were all circumcised, but many of them were not saved. In the end, although circumcised, they were treated as if they were not. This is because they did not keep God's law and love God and their neighbour as themselves. They were a law unto themselves.

But that does not mean that the Lord God now wanted to do away with circumcision. No, for to the Israelites circumcision was connected to the promises. God commanded Abraham and his offspring to be circumcised; with it, he attached the promises of earthly and eternal blessings. And those promises were received by the children through the parents.

Blessings

It is a great blessing that we, as believers, may have our children baptized and that parents can bring them to the baptismal font. What a blessing for our children to receive the sign and seal of the covenant and receive God's promise that they may be saved through the gospel.

Of course, a baptized baby doesn't understand any of that yet. But the parents promise to bring their child up in the knowledge of God's wonderful promises to the believers and their seed. As family, they belong to God's covenant people.

In that regard, there is no difference between the Old Testament and the New Testament children. The inclusion in both the Old and New Testaments is through familial solidarity. In other words, through the families. And the covenant is not just about belonging to an ethnic community. That was indeed an essential element in the Old Testament. Then, circumcision made you part of the Jewish people. But the covenant we have now is new, as we read in Hebrews 8:13. Now there is a greater inclusion. Now, families from all kinds of nations may receive those same promises already made to Abraham, the father of all believers.

How exactly are you included? How does that work within a family? We read in 1 Corinthians 7:14 that even if only one parent is a believer, their child is considered holy, that is, sanctified (holiness and sanctification refer to the same thing).

But it says the same thing about an unbelieving partner. It states that if one of the partners in a marriage is an unbeliever, then they are sanctified, made holy, through the other.

Isn't that amazing? How can an unbeliever be holy? Well, because of the Christian family to which that person belongs! For you must understand sanctification here in the proper sense, according to the original meaning of that word.

The primary meaning of sanctification is that you have been set apart from the world. And that happens within a marriage, even if one of the partners is an unbeliever. How so? The believing partner will try to bring the unbelieving partner into contact with the gospel as much as possible through mealtime devotions, prayer, and other means.

In this way, the unbelieving partner is given a privileged position in this sinful world. That unbelieving partner is continually brought into contact with the gospel of salvation.

We usually understand sanctification as referring to the Holy Spirit's outward and inward work. But it can also refer exclusively to the outward working of the Holy Spirit. And that is what the sense is here in 1 Corinthians 7:14. That is what happens to an unbelieving partner, and that is also what happens to a child. Baptism, as such, does not regenerate you. But it does alert you that you have been set apart and are constantly brought into contact with the gospel of salvation through those whom the Lord has put in your path, especially your family.

The Importance of Family

That is why families are so important: they bring you into contact with the glorious Gospel of salvation. And that is why the Lord God also says that he blesses in the generations (Genesis 17:1-8; Psalm 128; Acts 2:39, etc.). In the New Testament, there are twelve references to people who were baptized. But note that a quarter of them were baptized as part of a household. Those who hold to adult baptism state that likely there were no young children in those households and that, for that reason, we cannot prove anything by this. They say that ours is an argument from silence. That's true.

But what a pregnant silence that is!

How likely would it be that no little children were included in those households that were baptized? Highly unlikely. Not only that but nowhere do we see in the New Testament that now, suddenly, children are no longer included in the covenant community. Why would children who formerly in the Old Testament were included in the covenant and received God's promises no longer be included in the New?

If there was such a change, don't you think a big deal would have been made of this? Surely, the Jews who were converted to Christianity would have challenged this, and both Jesus and his disciples would have explained that change. There is no mention of such a change in the status of children in the New Testament.

Another argument Baptists will make is that not only is there no mention of infant baptism in the New Testament, but there is also no mention of infant baptism in the history of the early church.

To be sure, they admit that the well-known theologian Origen mentions infant baptism and wrote, "According to the usage of the church, baptism is given even to infants" (*Commentary on Romans*, Book 5, Ch. 9). But they dismiss the significance of that statement since this was written in AD 250, some two hundred years after Christ, and assert that within that timeframe somehow the baptism of children must have become the practice. They say that the church changed things during that timeframe. They went from the baptism of adults only to the baptism of children as well. Such a change came about over those two hundred years.

Do you really think that if the early Christian church had gone from the baptism of adults to the baptism of infants during those two hundred years, there would have been no mention of that in the writings of the church fathers? That there would be no written records of that?

Many documents from the second and third centuries after Christ about important doctrinal discussions were found. Think about the discussion about the Trinity. That issue had been brewing for close to two hundred years. Finally, in AD 325, after the persecution of Christians had ended, the churches came together to refute the heresies that had been floating around for these many years. There are all kinds of documents dealing with those critical doctrinal issues. And yet, you do not find anywhere any change about the baptism of infants.

Why not? Because there was no change. Children were always included in the covenant, just like they were in the Old Testament. They were included through their parents. If that doctrine had been changed, there would have been many discussions.

It is good that we did not throw out the baby with the bathwater as the Anabaptists did during the Reformation. God blesses in and through the generations. He blesses little children through the parents who bring them up with the knowledge of God's promises.

Hence, the substantial presence of people of all ages is evident within churches that hold a sincere commitment to the practice of child baptism. It is a blessing to witness the church gathering of great-grandparents, grandparents, parents, children, and even the little ones as covenant community.

Indeed, it would be great if there were more adult baptisms in those churches. We could use some of the zeal of evangelicals to bring God's Word to whomever and wherever we can. It's good to observe the enthusiasm with which numerous individuals in our churches reach out to non-believers and those who have drifted from the gospel.

But, let us not do that at the expense of the covenant through familial association and become individualistic in our approach. When you do that, there is no strong commitment to a church community as such, and people come and go constantly. That is why in adult baptism-only churches, children are more likely to walk away from God and his church, for the church and the parents leave it up to their children to come to God through faith.

No, God uses the parents and the covenant community as

instruments in his hands to give you faith. There must be a strong bond between the members of the covenant. As a covenant community, we do not walk away from each other so easily. We are family. We are committed to each other and love each other.

God greatly blesses us through the covenant he established with us as believers and our seed. We are blessed not because of who we are but because of God and who he is. It is all his doing. And in his wisdom, he blesses in the generations.

Be faithful to his promises and keenly aware of his demands. Give thanks to him for salvation through no merit of your own. Give thanks to him through the generations. Then, the Lord will also bless you through the generations and bless us as his covenant community.

Reflection

1. In what ways do you find joy and hope in knowing that God has made you part of his family and that he loves you like an earthly father loves his child? Take time to reflect on the many ways that God's fatherly love shows in your life and the lives of your loved ones.

2. Romans 14:8 states, "For if we live, we live to the Lord, and if we die, we die to the Lord. So then, whether we live or whether we die, we are the Lord's." What comfort do you have in knowing that you, both body and soul, belong to God?

Chapter 5
Born Again?

*"Blessed be the God and Father of our Lord Jesus
Christ!
According to his great mercy,
he has caused us to be born again to a living hope
through the resurrection of Jesus Christ
from the dead,"*
(1 Peter 1:3)

*"For in one Spirit we were all baptized into one body—
Jews or Greeks, slaves or free—and all were made to
drink of one Spirit."*
(1 Corinthians 12:13)

Introduction

The birth of a child is a remarkable event in both a family's and a church's life. Each time a child is born, we witness the wondrous miracle of the gift of life. While the process of childbirth holds some mysteries, we do possess a comprehensive understanding of how and when it occurs.

John 3 also deals with birth, not physical birth but spiritual birth, which is an even greater miracle brought about by the Holy Spirit. However, many of us are unsure when and how that happens.

Exactly when are you reborn? At what point in your life do you have the Holy Spirit? Does a baby have the Holy Spirit already from birth? And how exactly do you receive the Holy Spirit? Do you receive the Holy Spirit because you were born into a Christian family? Is that an automatic thing? And how do you know that you have the Holy Spirit? How can you be sure?

One thing we do know, however, is that, as Jesus says to Nicodemus, you cannot enter the kingdom of God unless you are born again (John 3:5). But when the Lord Jesus speaks these words, he speaks to an adult. How can you apply that to children?

And so many questions need answers. In this chapter, we are going to look at the great news about the miraculous work of the Holy Spirit. We will see that our rebirth is, first, initiated by the Holy Spirit, second, confirmed in God's covenant, and finally, controlled by God.

Scripture

John 3:1–21

Now there was a man of the Pharisees named Nicodemus, a ruler of the Jews.

2 This man came to Jesus by night and said to him, "Rabbi, we know that you are a teacher come from God, for no one can do these signs that you do unless God is with him."

3 Jesus answered him, "Truly, truly, I say to you, unless one is born again he cannot see the kingdom of God."

4 Nicodemus said to him, "How can a man be born when he is old? Can he enter a second time into his mother's womb and be born?"

5 Jesus answered, "Truly, truly, I say to you, unless one is born of water and the Spirit, he cannot enter the kingdom of God.

6 That which is born of the flesh is flesh, and that which is born of the Spirit is spirit.

7 Do not marvel that I said to you, 'You must be born again.'

8 The wind blows where it wishes, and you hear its sound, but you do not know where it comes from or where it goes. So it is with everyone who is born of the Spirit."

9 Nicodemus said to him, "How can these things be?"

10 Jesus answered him, "Are you the teacher of Israel and yet you do not understand these things?

11 Truly, truly, I say to you, we speak of what we know, and bear witness to what we have seen, but you do not receive our testimony.

12 If I have told you earthly things and you do not believe, how can you believe if I tell you heavenly things?

13 No one has ascended into heaven except he who descended from heaven, the Son of Man.

14 And as Moses lifted up the serpent in the wilderness, so must the Son of Man be lifted up,

15 that whoever believes in him may have eternal life.

16 "For God so loved the world, that he gave his only Son, that whoever believes in him should not perish but have eternal life.

17 For God did not send his Son into the world to condemn the world, but in order that the world might be saved through him.

18 Whoever believes in him is not condemned, but whoever does not believe is condemned already, because he has not believed in the name of the only Son of God.

19 And this is the judgment: the light has come into the world, and people loved the darkness rather than the light because their works were evil.

20 For everyone who does wicked things hates the light and does not come to the light, lest his works should be exposed.

21 But whoever does what is true comes to the light, so that it may be clearly seen that his works have been carried out in God."

Rebirth

Our Rebirth is Initiated by the Holy Spirit

It is noteworthy how the Lord Jesus came to speak about being born again. The issue came about because of a question from a man named Nicodemus. He was a Pharisee and, as such, a prominent leader in Israel who was perplexed about who Jesus truly is. He observed the miracles Jesus was performing, saw the excitement that he stirred up amongst the people, and wanted to know more about him. As a result, he approached Jesus under the cover of nightfall.

Some say Nicodemus came to Jesus at night because he did not want the other Pharisees to know he was coming to see him and wanted to keep it secret. However, the text does not say that. It just mentions that he came at night. It could well be that he came at night because, at night, you have fewer interruptions, and it is easier to have a lengthy and deep-going discussion, which is what Nicodemus wanted, for he was struggling with something quite profound. He was a devout man and took his relationship with God seriously.

That is why the ministry of Jesus was so troubling to him. Nicodemus wondered whether Jesus was the Messiah, the Anointed One they had been waiting for. He did not directly ask Jesus whether he was the Messiah, but the Lord Jesus could see that that was the question in his heart.

Instead of addressing that issue, Jesus takes an entirely different tack. He does not confirm or deny that he is the Messiah. He could have done that. He could have quoted the Old Testament and shown Nicodemus how everything in the Old Testament points to his coming and how it is now being fulfilled. He could have pointed to the miracles he is doing and to all the other signs that show him to be the Messiah, the Son of God.

He does not do that. Why not? Because Jesus knows that it would not make any difference in the mind of Nicodemus. If you want to understand who the Messiah is, you cannot come to that understanding through logical analysis. Not that logic and reason are excluded. Not at all. But ultimately, it is always a matter of faith. It is a matter of the inclination of the heart. If you don't want to believe something, you won't, no matter what evidence is presented. Faith and reason must go together.

We are not any different today. For example, we can all observe the miracle of creation. We can clearly see how this wonderful creation could never ever have come about by chance, by evolution. The evidence of a mighty Creator is overwhelming. And yet, most people do not believe.

Why is that? Because they don't want to be bothered to find the truth. You can come with all the evidence in the world, but if they do not want to accept that God has made everything, then whatever you say to them makes no difference. They won't believe it. It is always a matter of faith. It's always a matter of the heart, of submission to God, and of following his agenda, not yours.

Jesus wants to open Nicodemus's eyes to the real truth and speaks to him about being born again. And what he says to him is quite significant and noteworthy. That is clear from how he introduces what he is about to say. He begins by saying, "Truly, truly, I say to you." In Greek it says, "Amen, amen, I say to you." You must pay close attention whenever the Lord Jesus uses these words. He is about to teach you something quite astonishing.

And then come the crucial words: "No one can see the kingdom of God unless he is born again." Nicodemus's ultimate concern was the kingdom. He wanted to be part of God's kingdom and to know if Jesus is the long-awaited Messiah, the Anointed One from the Lord God who holds the key to the kingdom of heaven.

Jesus understands that. That, ultimately, is what motivates all of us. By nature, we are concerned first about ourselves and our place in God's kingdom. For us, the question is, too, "Will I go to heaven when I die? Am I going to enjoy all the wonderful blessings of the life hereafter?" Nicodemus is after those ultimate answers.

But now Jesus says you cannot see the kingdom unless you are born again. Note well that he uses the words "*to see* the kingdom" in verse 3, whereas, in verse 5, he speaks about *entering* the kingdom. That is because there is a progression in view here. You must first open your eyes and see the kingdom. You must perceive it. You must understand what God's kingdom is all about. You must be consciously aware of who the King is and who the citizens of that kingdom are. Only then can you come to an understanding as to how you enter the kingdom.

And so, what's God's kingdom all about? Well, God's kingdom is first of all a *spiritual* kingdom. Rather than having a horizontal understanding, we need to have a vertical understanding. We must fix our eyes above where God is in heaven. That is why Jesus uses a Greek word, *ánōthen*, that has two meanings. The way most translations render what the Lord Jesus says is that you must be "born *again*." But that same word, *ánōthen*, can also just as easily be translated as "above." You must be born "from *above*." That is why in a footnote (ESV: "or *from above*; the Greek is purposely ambiguous and can mean both *again* and *from above*; also verse

86

7") many translations give that as a possible translation.

In other words, rebirth does not come about because of your decision. No, it comes about from above because of something that God does. He has to initiate your rebirth.

Our Rebirth is Confirmed in God's Covenant

It is important to understand the tradition of Nicodemus. As a Pharisee, he is deeply concerned about his entrance into the kingdom. But he thinks that the way in is through work righteousness. Entrance is through something you *do*, or because of who you *are*. The Pharisees are proud that they are descended from Abraham and, therefore, God's special people, for God made the promises to Abraham and his descendants. And so, the matter of the kingdom for them is, first, a birthright and, secondly, something to which you personally contribute.

But that is not the way into God's kingdom. It is something much more profound, much more wonderful and reassuring. Oh sure, the descendants of Abraham are God's special covenant children. But not everyone who is descended from Abraham will be saved. On the contrary. Why are they God's special people? Only because he, out of all the other nations, chose to proclaim his Word to them, to Israel. He revealed himself to that people. He came to them with the ten words of the covenant on Mount Sinai. He sent his prophets to that nation. Out of his own free will, he chose that nation.

But many of God's people rejected God's covenant and did not keep his commandments. They walked away from the covenant because they did not want to listen to the prophets and, consequently, not to the greatest prophet of all, the Lord Jesus Christ.

And so, there is more to the question of entrance into heaven than just being part of God's special people. It is not just a matter of a physical bond with God and his people but of a spiritual bond.

As we saw in Chapter 4, that is also the case with children of believing parents. When such parents have their children baptized, they do so because they believe that they are God's covenant children and, as such, are set apart from the world.

What makes them so special? Do they have certain qualities that other children do not have? No. It's only because of God's love. In his great love, he gave them parents who belong to God's covenant. He gave them parents who will teach their children as they grow up in the ways of the Lord.

They will teach them about God's wonderful covenant, about his promises and his demands, for that is what faithful Christian parents promise to do at the time of their children's baptism. They will read to them daily from the Bible at the supper table. As soon as their children can sit still long enough without making a disturbance, they will take them to church. If possible, they will ensure their children receive a Christian education and have Christian friends.

You see, those things make our children special, holy even. As Paul says in 1 Corinthians 7:14, children of a believing parent are not unclean but holy. Holiness has to do with cleanliness and being set apart. It has to do with being washed with the Word. That's also what the Lord Jesus refers to when he says in John 15:3, "You are already clean because of the word I have spoken to you."

Ultimately, then, children of believing parents are special people because of the Word of God that is given to them. It has nothing to do with any personal attributes. It was not so either that the nation Israel was such a fine people that the Lord chose them.

Israel was not any better or more worthy than the other nations around them.

That is also how it is with God's people today. Parents who bring their children to the baptismal font are not any better than anyone else. They are sinners like all other human beings.

They are not worthy of themselves, except for one thing: in his mercy, God has revealed his Word to them. And now they believe. And even that faith is a gift from God (Ephesians 2:8). God wants us to realize that we have nothing of ourselves to boast about. God is in control.

Does that mean that baptism saves you? No. If a covenant child of God has come of age and wants nothing to do with the Word of God, walking away from him and his people, then, despite all the instruction received, such a person has rejected the Word of God. Such a person can no longer be considered to be a citizen of God's kingdom. And they can only blame themselves for that.

Although God establishes the covenant unilaterally, it is bilateral in its existence. In other words, God also wants you to do something, namely, to choose for him. The Lord also gave his people Israel the choice just before they entered the promised land and told them they must choose whom they will serve, whether the gods of the foreign nations or him (Joshua 24:7).

But in the final analysis, it is not you who makes the choice. The Lord God does. This is a mystery and hard for us to understand. How can it be that, on the one hand, we must make a choice, and on the other hand, it is God who chooses us? Well, that is what the Scriptures tell us. In John 6:44, Jesus says, "No one can come to me unless the Father who sent me draws him. And I will raise him up on the last day." The point is that we can do nothing without God. Although he gives us the ability to make choices, we are still dependent on him as we do so.

He comes to his special people, including the children, with his beautiful promises. He does that already before they understand anything at all. He doesn't make a covenant with anyone because of their faith or anything they do. No, he makes a covenant with them despite the great sinners they are, and despite the great sinners their children are.

That is also what Jesus is trying to tell Nicodemus. Nicodemus, however, appears not to get the picture. That is why he asks, "How can a man be born when he is old? Can he enter a second time into his mother's womb and be born?" (John 3:4).

Don't think, however, that Nicodemus doesn't understand what Jesus is driving at. He knows the Scriptures. He knows from the Old Testament Scriptures that the Lord God does not just deal with the flesh but especially with the heart. But Nicodemus is digging further. He wants to know what man's role is in all this. He wants Jesus to elaborate. And that's precisely what Jesus does. He says, "Truly, truly, I say to you, unless one is born of water and the Spirit, he cannot enter the kingdom of God" (John 3:5).

Again, he emphasizes that this is God's doing. Nicodemus understands that when Jesus says that you must be born of water, he is speaking about the water of baptism. Nicodemus knew what baptism was about. It has to do with cleansing. The Pharisees themselves required it from any Gentile who was converted to Judaism. They had to be circumcised and baptized before they were considered to be part of God's people and allowed to enter the temple in Jerusalem.

Jesus, however, connects this cleansing ritual with the Spirit. The Holy Spirit washes you and makes you clean and holy. You cannot separate the Holy Spirit from the cleansing. It is God's doing.

Our Rebirth is Controlled by God

"But when exactly does that happen?" you may ask. "Has it happened to me?" Please notice how Lord Jesus explains the mystery of God's working to Nicodemus. He shows that he is always in control in every way. In verse 8, he compares the Spirit to the wind. In New Testament Greek (and in Old Testament Hebrew), there are two different words that you can use for wind. But the word that he uses here is the same word used for the Spirit. So, it was easy for Nicodemus and the original readers to make the immediate connection between wind or breath and Spirit.

He then reminds Nicodemus about its mysteriousness. You don't always feel the wind, and then suddenly, it starts blowing. And you don't always know where it comes from, either. It can blow this way or that way or not be perceptible at all.

Well, says Jesus, that's also how it is with the Spirit of God. You have no control over it. You don't know where it goes. It works mysteriously. But God does know. Just as he controls the wind, he also controls the Spirit. It's all his doing. Some are regenerated, and many are not. That is God's business. It is up to God to let his Spirit blow where he will.

One of the Reformed confessions, the Canons of Dort, summarizes this doctrine most beautifully: "This new creation . . . which God works in us without us . . . by no means . . . remains in the power of man. . . . It is, however, clearly a supernatural, most powerful, and at the same time most delightful, marvellous, mysterious, and inexpressible work" (Ch. 3 & 4, Art. 12). Further, "In this life believers cannot fully understand the way in which God does this work. Meanwhile, however, it is enough for them to know and experience that by this grace of God they believe with the heart and love their Saviour." (Art.13)

You will undoubtedly have some serious questions at this point. Isn't that unfair? And how do I know whether I have been reborn? How do I know that I have the Holy Spirit? Jesus compares the concept of birth to rebirth because there are many similarities, and the comparison aids our understanding.

Consider, how do parents know that their child is born? Well, that's obvious. They can see that with their eyes. They were there when that happened. And now their child is alive. And because they nurture that child, the child continues to grow and grow and grow. Within a few months, a baby will weigh double the amount at birth. That's because of the good food and love they will receive. And the child will continue to grow and grow until they become an adult.

The same is true of rebirth. How do children of God know they are born again? Well, first, they are alive in Christ. That is what Jesus said to children in his midst in Matthew 18 when he welcomed them and told his disciples that those little children belong to the kingdom of God. And so, to Jesus, a little child is a part of the kingdom of God.

And how do you know that further? Well, day in and day out, children of believers are being fed God's Word and, in this way, grow in their faith. They learn more and more about God and how they must conduct themselves.

The most important thing they learn about God is that they are his children, not because of their good behaviour, but despite their bad behaviour. God loves them unconditionally.

Isn't that the way it is with our own children as well? We don't tell our children that we will accept them as long as they accept us first. And we don't tell them either that they are our children because of their good behaviour. No. They are our children because they are our flesh and blood, which is why we also provide for them and give them everything they need. And we want to protect them from harm and give them instructions on how to live in this dangerous world.

That is how it works with us as God's children. He created us, gave birth to us, and loves us. We have a very strong bond with him. That is why he wants to protect us from harm and gives us his Ten Commandments. He gives them to us because of our relationship with him.

Therefore, rebirth is all about our relationship with him. If we did not have a relationship with him and if he had not initiated that relationship, we would be like the fallen angels, who stand utterly condemned. We are nothing without God.

And so, we must live lives of thankfulness to him. He promises to feed us and sustain us in all kinds of circumstances. He promises to be with us always, even in our darkest hours. He promises never to abandon us.

And so, if you know that wonderful God to be your God, do you then not want to live according to his will? Even though you will fall far short of the obedience that God requires from you, he promises to forgive you and give you eternal life. Indeed, if you believe in God, don't you then not want to live according to the law of God? Of course you do.

Isn't that the way we treat our children as well? We dearly love them and provide them with everything they need to have a good life. And we give them instructions on how to conduct themselves so that they do not come to harm.

Can you imagine if you said to your children, "I'm not going to love you and accept you as my child unless you first show that you believe in me and show that you are a good person who rarely does anything wrong?" You would not have a relationship with them. It is up to you as a parent to establish the relationship and to show how that functions.

You lovingly nurture the relationship that you have with your children, and you also nurture the relationship they have with their heavenly Father. You teach them about God and have them talk to the heavenly Father by teaching them to pray at night before they go to bed. You teach them the wonderful stories found in the Bible. And you teach them that when they do something wrong, they sin against God, and you teach them to ask for the forgiveness of their sins. You teach them to live out of God's promises and out of what he has done. And so, despite their sinfulness, they grow in the Lord and learn to love him.

In this way, we see that a child of believing parents receives the Holy Spirit already at birth. Those brought up in Christian homes slowly but surely grow in their knowledge and in their faith and thereby are daily regenerated—that is, they are reborn.

In such cases, there's no exact point where they can say they were reborn, whereas some people, especially those who come to faith at a later age, can give the exact date of their rebirth. They remember becoming new creatures when they heard the gospel of salvation. They went from one type of life to another. They went from being dead to being alive.

But again, please do not think this happens because of human effort. Also, when you come to faith at a later age, it is still in response to what God has done and does. Consider what the apostle Paul says in Ephesians 2:4-5: "But God, being rich in mercy, because of the great love with which he loved us, even when we were dead in our trespasses, made us alive together with Christ—by grace you have been saved—."

It is always God's doing. Ultimately, we respond to what God has done through his Son, Jesus Christ. The apostle Peter writes, "Blessed be the God and Father of our Lord Jesus Christ! According to his great mercy, he has caused us to be **born again** to a living hope through the resurrection of Jesus Christ from the dead." (1 Peter 1:3).

New birth is given to us because of the Lord Jesus Christ's resurrection for all who belong to him. Our rebirth was obtained long before we were born. And now, we must respond to that and claim that reality. That is true for children as well as for adults. Some respond to that later than others and differently. But our rebirth is never done because of our faith. It is based on what is done from above, by God the Holy Spirit.

So, when were you born again? At the time of the resurrection of the Lord Jesus Christ. But you must make this new life a reality in your life. By God's grace, the Holy Spirit has made you a new person who is able to live out of what God has done. Although we fail all the time, because of the promise of the forgiveness of sins and eternal life for all who believe, your life in Christ is a renewed and flourishing life. Ultimately, it is all his doing. To him be the glory.

Reflection

1. The ultimate question of Nicodemus was about the kingdom of God and his own place in it. Jesus tells him that you cannot be part of the kingdom of God unless you are born again. How can we know if we are born again?

2. In what ways does physical birth resemble spiritual birth? How are those similarities evident in your life?

Chapter 6
Our Search for the Comfort of Home

"How lovely is your dwelling place, O LORD of hosts!
My soul longs, yes, faints for the courts of the LORD;
my heart and flesh sing for joy to the living God.
Even the sparrow finds a home,
and the swallow a nest for herself,
where she may lay her young, at your altars,
O LORD of hosts, my King and my God.
Blessed are those who dwell in your house, ever
singing your praise!"
Psalm 84:1–4

Introduction

Home, that's where we are most comfortable. There, we are surrounded by beloved family and material things that are dear and familiar to us. That's where we know where we can find what we need and where we have access to a place where we belong. When we are at home, we feel free. That's where we have our favourite chair, our own bed, and our own possessions. That's where we are also surrounded by loved ones with whom we are comfortable. That's where we can speak our minds, be ourselves, and feel secure and safe.

When you're away from home, then you miss your familiar

surroundings. And so, it is hard to be away from home, especially for children. The further children are away from home and the less familiar the place they are in is, the harder it is. And the longer they are gone from home, the more miserable they feel.

The Heidelberg Catechism deals with our sin and misery. In the original German edition, the word *elend* is used. It means "out of the land." And so essentially, it means "away from home." Misery has to do with being away from home.

When she was well into her eighties, my mother was reminiscing about her younger years and told me about the time when she was twenty-five years old and engaged to be married. She was still living at home. (In those days, you did not leave home until you were married. It just wasn't done, and you also couldn't afford it.)

But once, she had a falling out with her mom and dad. Her fiancé's mother had broken her neck and was on her deathbed. Her fiancé wanted her to come with him to the hospital to visit her. But even though my mother was an adult, her parents did not allow her to go. For she still had chores to do. When you lived at home, you were expected to pull your weight. But she went anyway. Her fiancé insisted, for that might be the last time she could speak to her fiancé's mother.

Her parents, especially her mother, were angry with her for defying them. Because she disobeyed them, she could no longer come home. She was no longer welcome, nor was her fiancé. Most of her brothers and sisters even sided with her parents. Her mother was a hard woman who did not tolerate dissent.

While she was away from home, my mother was miserable. She did not like it that she had a falling out with her parents. She missed the comforts of home. After about three or four months, she talked to her dad and told him, even though she was not at fault, that she was sorry about the quarrel, and she asked him if she was allowed to come home again. He embraced her and said, "Of course. We missed you."

So, difficult as it was, she went home again and reconciled herself to her mother. It was worth it to her, for despite everything, she still loved her parents. And her parents also loved her. Being away from each other made them feel miserable, driving them again into each other's arms.

That's also the way it is with our heavenly Father. Except, when it comes to our relationship with him, it is totally our own fault. Knowing our sins and misery must teach us to want to be home with him.

In Chapter 2, we learned that Adam and Eve, because of their rebellion and sin, were banished from the beautiful home that God had provided for them. Because of sin, God's creation became subject to decay and death and still today this world is subject to all kinds of turmoil and misery. Thankfully, God has created the desire within us to seek a better world. However, our striving to overcome the ravages that plague this world will come to nothing if the Lord Jesus is not part of the solution. Only he can reconcile us to God and his creation and to each other.

In this chapter, we will see that God wants us to desire to be with him and enjoy the eternal riches he has prepared for those who believe in him.

Scripture

Luke 15:11–24

The Parable of the Prodigal Son

11 And he said, "There was a man who had two sons.

12 And the younger of them said to his father, 'Father, give me the share of property that is coming to me.' And he divided his property between them.

13 Not many days later, the younger son gathered all he had and took a journey into a far country, and there he squandered his property in reckless living.

14 And when he had spent everything, a severe famine arose in that country, and he began to be in need.

15 So he went and hired himself out to one of the citizens of that country, who sent him into his fields to feed pigs.

16 And he was longing to be fed with the pods that the pigs ate, and no one gave him anything.

17 "But when he came to himself, he said, 'How many of my father's hired servants have more than enough bread, but I perish here with hunger!

18 I will arise and go to my father, and I will say to him, "Father, I have sinned against heaven and before you.

19 I am no longer worthy to be called your son. Treat me as one of your hired servants."'

20 And he arose and came to his father. But while he was still a long way off, his father saw him and felt compassion, and ran and embraced him and kissed him.

21 And the son said to him, 'Father, I have sinned against heaven and before you. I am no longer worthy to be called your son.'

22 But the father said to his servants, 'Bring quickly the best robe, and put it on him, and put a ring on his hand, and shoes on his feet.

23 And bring the fattened calf and kill it, and let us eat and celebrate.

24 For this my son was dead, and is alive again; he was lost, and is found.' And they began to celebrate.

Matthew 19:16–26

The Rich Young Man

16 And behold, a man came up to him, saying, "Teacher, what good deed must I do to have eternal life?"

17 And he said to him, "Why do you ask me about what is good? There is only one who is good. If you would enter life, keep the commandments."

18 He said to him, "Which ones?" And Jesus said, "You shall not murder, You shall not commit adultery, You shall not steal, You shall not bear false witness,

19 Honor your father and mother, and, You shall love your neighbor as yourself."

20 The young man said to him, "All these I have kept. What do I still lack?"

21 Jesus said to him, "If you would be perfect, go, sell what you possess and give to the poor, and you will have treasure in heaven; and come, follow me."

22 When the young man heard this he went away sorrowful, for he had great possessions.

23 And Jesus said to his disciples, "Truly, I say to you, only with difficulty will a rich person enter the kingdom of heaven.

24 Again I tell you, it is easier for a camel to go through the eye of a needle than for a rich person to enter the kingdom of God."

25 When the disciples heard this, they were greatly astonished, saying, "Who then can be saved?"

26 But Jesus looked at them and said, "With man this is impossible, but with God all things are possible."

Heidelberg Catechism

3.　Q.　From where do you know
　　　　your sins and misery?

　　　A.　From the law of God.[1]

　　　[1] Rom 3:20; 7:7–25.

4.　Q.　What does God's law require of us?

　　　A.　Christ teaches us this in a summary in Matthew 22:

　　　　You shall love the Lord your God
　　　　with all your heart
　　　　and with all your soul
　　　　and with all your mind.[1]
　　　　This is the great and first commandment.
　　　　And a second is like it:
　　　　You shall love your neighbour as yourself.
　　　　On these two commandments depend
　　　　all the Law and the Prophets.[2]

　　　[1] Deut 6:5.
　　　[2] Lev 19:18.

5.　Q.　Can you keep all this perfectly?

　　　A.　No[1], I am inclined by nature
　　　　to hate God and my neighbour.[2]

　　　[1] Rom 3:10, 23; 1 Jn 1:8, 10.
　　　[2] Gen 6:5; 8:21; Jer 17:9; Rom 7:23; 8:7; Eph 2:3; Tit 3:3.

Sin and Misery

The catechism, which is a summary of God's Word, tells us that we know our sins and misery from the law of God. What does that mean? This can be easily misunderstood and abused. We could, for example, use the law as a checklist, just like a mechanic has a checklist to see how roadworthy a car is. He will check the tires to see if there is enough tread left. And then the brakes. Is there enough brake fluid? If not, he'll top it up. And he will check the oil. Is it low? Does it need changing? And what about the timing belt? And what about the other belts? Are they tight enough? Are they fraying? And so forth. And so he has a checklist to ensure everything is in good working order. If not, then it must be fixed first. Only then will it be roadworthy.

Some people think that the law is such a checklist as well: "How well am I doing in the keeping of the law? Let me see, is God number one in my life? I regularly attend church, pray, read the Bible, and do my best to lead a Christian lifestyle. Check. And what about using God's name in vain? Well, I never blaspheme. I don't curse like the people at work. Check. And stealing? I don't do that either. I'm also faithful to my marriage partner. I don't cheat. Oh sure, I'm not perfect in any of these things. But I'm sure a lot better than most others. I think I'm okay."

That is how the rich young man in the Matthew passage used the law, as a checklist. He had examined himself and concluded that he did not murder, did not commit adultery, did not steal, and did not give false testimony, honours his father and his mother and loves his neighbour as himself. "All these commandments I have kept," the young man said to the Lord Jesus. "What do I still lack?" He wanted a pat on the back from Jesus and to be commended for what he had done.

However, that's work righteousness and goes against Scripture. It goes radically against what the Gospel is all about. It says in Romans 3:10, "As it is written: 'None is righteous, no, not one.'"

And yet, that is how we all tend to look at the law. We always want to return to the idea that we can earn a place with our Father in heaven because of something we have done. Because of our pride, we want to be able to contribute, in one way or the other, to our own salvation. We are always thinking of ways to escape our predicament because of our sins. We know we are guilty, but then we want to find a way out without truly repenting from our sins.

Just imagine if the lost son in the Luke passage had done the same. Suppose he only wanted to get out of the tight spot he got himself into. He says to himself, "Look at what I've done. I've squandered the money my father has given me, and now I'm in deep trouble. What can I do? I have nothing left. Anything is better than what I have now. And so, let me find a way to get back into my father's home. At least then I'll have a square meal every day. Even if I have to keep some of the rules of the house as people watch me, I'll do it. I'll go through the motions. It'll be worth it."

If that is the attitude he had, then he never really repented. Then he would not have had a change of heart, for he would still be using his father for his own selfish ends. The only reason he would want to go back home would be to get himself out of a difficult situation. He would only be opportunistic.

The same thing is true of the rich young man. Note well the question that he is asking the Lord Jesus. He asks him what good thing he must do to get eternal life. He only thinks about what he can get for himself. That's his only interest. It's only about external obedience.

That is why the catechism in Answer 4 is right on the money. It doesn't give you a list of dos and don'ts. It doesn't come with this commandment and that commandment and with this rule and that rule. No, it tells you about love. It tells you that you must love God and your neighbour.

Here we come to the heart of the matter, literally and figuratively. Keeping the law is not about you or me; it is not about how we can earn ourselves a place in heaven. No, it is about our relationship with God and with our neighbour.

Imagine if all you're concerned about in your own home is your personal comfort and well-being. You don't care about anybody else. It doesn't matter to you that you deny others their comfort and their rights. No, you want the best things of home for yourself. And so, you do whatever you feel like. You only contribute by doing the bare minimum. You just go through the motions.

You can well imagine that such an attitude will cause all kinds of friction in the home. Your parents, your husband or wife, will soon get on your case, for your heart is not in it. You love yourself more than you love anybody else.

No doubt they will be angry with you. And this will show in their angry or disappointed faces.

Ultimately, you do not learn your misery by looking at the law, but by looking at the Lawgiver, your Father in heaven. When you look him in the face (by reading and meditating on his Word), you will see the disappointment on his face, and you will realize how selfish you are in the way you behave.

Ultimately, you learn your sins and misery by looking at the Lord Jesus Christ. He teaches you. That is also what we read in Galatians 3:24, namely that "the law was our guardian until Christ came, in order that we might be justified by faith."

The Bible teaches us that only because of God's love can we have comfort in our Father's home (John 14:1, 2; Revelation 21:3, 4). Only because of him can we access all the riches found in our Father's home, for we belong to him with body and soul. Our older brother, the Lord Jesus, bought us with his precious blood. In this way, he made us part of God's family again.

You first must realize the love of God through the Lord Jesus

Christ. It is only then that you can see your own sins. When you look at him, you have to ask yourself, "Why did he have to die? Why did he have to empty himself of the glory he had with his Father in heaven? Why did he have to give up the comforts of his heavenly home? And why did he have to allow himself to be forsaken by God? Why did his Father in heaven have to push him away from him? He was an innocent man."

In time the answer becomes clear: it is because of my sin, my inability to do any good. Christ is the one who kept the law for us. Once you see the wonderful things he has done for us and his great love for us, you also realize what we have done and how far we have wandered away from home. When we come to that realization, we will say, "Father, I have sinned against heaven and against you. I am no longer worthy to be called your son" (Luke 15:18).

Wandering Away from Home

Why did we wander away from home in the first place? What was the reason? Well, we must go back to Paradise, to Adam and Eve. The Lord God had given them a most beautiful home. They had everything there they could possibly want.

But then they sinned. They wanted more. They wanted to go their own way. They thought only about themselves and not about their Father in heaven, who supplied them with everything they had. As a result, they spoiled the atmosphere in their home. And because of that, they had to be ousted.

That has been the case ever since. It is still our nature to want to please ourselves at the expense of our relationship with God and our relationship with our neighbour. That is why the catechism says that we hate God and our neighbour.

Perhaps you think that that is a bit exaggerated. But there's much more to this than we are willing to admit. We may even sympathize with the younger son in Luke 15:11–24. We may think, "Oh sure, he grabbed the opportunity to try to make it on his own. But, isn't that a natural thing to do? Don't we all want our independence? Perhaps he should not have squandered his money the way he did, spending it on prostitutes and high living. But, was that the worst sin? Don't we all do stupid things at times, especially when we are young? Was that all that terrible?" No, it wasn't. But what he actually did was much worse than that.

Think about it. He said in effect, "Father, as far as I'm concerned, you can drop dead. You're nothing to me." You may think that is an exaggeration, but that is how it was. The only thing that tied him to his father was his father's money. For the rest, he didn't care about him. His heart was cold. He cared only about himself and his own pleasures.

But then, in the end, thankfully, he realizes what he has done. He humbles himself and says, "*I am no longer worthy to be called your son*" (Luke 15:19). And that's true. That's precisely how it was, for he had severed all ties with home.

That's also the picture God wants us to have of our own sins. The fact that we have sinned means that we have severed our ties with the Lord God. It's something we do time and again. When we sin, we place God outside of our lives. Then, it is as if he is dead to us.

That is why we must be called back. We have to repent. We must be called home again and again, for we continue to walk away from home. And before we know it, we could end up in a ditch someplace . . . or worse.

Don't we walk away from our Father in heaven all the time?

107

We do not want to keep the rules. We want to create our own comfort. We want to provide for ourselves.

But if you realize what it means to be away from the Father, far from home, then you know that you can be happy only with him. For your true riches lie with him. Your true riches are not found here on earth.

That is the mistake that the rich young man made. He only thought about himself and his earthly comforts. He did not want to give them up. The terrible thing is that he did not realize the true riches that he rejected, the true riches that he could find only by following the Lord Jesus all the way.

One of the hardest things for us is to examine ourselves and to realize our own misery. We look at how well we are doing in this life and are quite satisfied with ourselves. That is because we look just at the periphery of how we function in society. We look at the outside and conclude that we are functioning quite well, thank you very much. Oh sure, we have our moments, but by and large, we are not such bad people. We do what we need to do and get along with most people quite well.

But to realize your sins you must go deeper. You have to look inside yourself, in your heart. And if you truly examine your heart, then you also see the dark side of your heart. Then you see how your temper, your impatience, how you treat others, your irritability, your judgmental attitude, your selfishness and greediness hurt your relationship with others, especially your relationship with the Lord God.

We are very observant when it comes to the behaviour of others. We really feel it when they step on our toes and the toes of others. We clearly see how selfish such people who do that are and how they do not take others, especially ourselves, into consideration. It is easy for us to be critical of others.

But when it comes to ourselves, we are often blind to our own behaviour. Some people never really reach inside their own hearts to see how they behave and how others see them. They keep enacting the same selfish behaviours yet go around as if they truly understand their relationship with God and with our neighbour. They are blind. They never look inside themselves. It is as if they have an impenetrable steel plate in their heads. They do not understand that it is a matter of the heart.

But that is what God demands from us. He wants us to realize our miserable condition. He wants us to realize how far we have walked away from him. When you are away from your Father, you experience misery in the most profound sense.

That is the way it was with king David. In Psalm 32, he writes that because of his unconfessed sin, his bones wasted away through his groaning all day long. Day and night, he felt God's heavy hand on him. His strength, he said, was sapped as in the heat of summer. Talk about misery. That's how he felt when he no longer experienced God's presence.

But he was allowed to come home. When he realized how he had sinned against God, and after he confessed his sins from the heart, God again opened the door to him. He rejoiced. He writes in Psalm 32:7, "You are my hiding place; you will protect me from trouble and surround me with songs of deliverance" (NIV84). At home with God, he felt safe. He felt protected. He felt wanted. He once again experienced the joy of salvation.

When you realize your sins and your misery, and when you confess your sins, then the Lord God opens his arms to you, just like the father did in the parable of the lost son. When the son came home, no guard in front of the door said, "What are you doing here? You no longer belong here." No, his father personally opened the door wide to him.

That's also the way it is for us. Our Father in heaven also opens the door to us. And he does that time and again, for we walk away from him all the time. We sin against him day in and day out. But he forgives us our sins every time and opens the door wide.

And you know who that door is, don't you? That door is the Lord Jesus Christ. He says about himself, "I am the door. If anyone enters by me, he will be saved and will go in and out and find pasture" (John 10:9). The door is the Lord Jesus Christ. Because of him and through him, we may enter.

Isn't it a great miracle that we may come home time and again? Doesn't that show God's great love for us?

We have to realize how rich we are in God's home. We may not wander away, not first of all because of the riches he gives us but because of the relationship that he has established with us. It is about God's love for us and our love for him.

The Lord God wants us to be home with him. And he has done everything possible to make that happen. Nothing stands in the way except that we, too, must *want* to be home with him. We must believe that he is a loving heavenly Father who likes nothing better than having his children around him.

And so, believe. Believe God's sure promises that he will be a Father to all who want to be in his presence. And then the Lord will call you home, home forever.

Reflection

1. What is the one thing that will satisfy you in every way? What do you long for in this life? Do you think it is attainable and that it will last?

2. We all feel miserable at times. How do you overcome your misery? Read Philippians 4:4–13. Pray for a heart that is so fully satisfied with God and the home that he provides for all those who believe in him that you are able to be at peace, no matter what circumstances you find yourself in.

Chapter 7
What It Means to Be a Member
of God's Church

*"So we, though many, are one body in Christ,
and individually members one of another."*
Romans 12:5

*"The function of the church
is to bring people to Christ
and to bring Christ to the people."*
D. Martyn Lloyd-Jones

*"The church is not a social club,
but a training ground for discipleship."*
Oswald Chambers

Introduction

Have you ever wondered why there are so many different churches? Is that normal? And if it is, why? Some people are fine with the variety of churches; they like having options. If you do not like one church, you can go to another. People should be able to choose whatever church they want to attend, right? You should be able to go to a church where you feel you fit in and where the people are most like you. You shouldn't have to deal with people who bother you and whose values are different from yours. God doesn't really care which church you go to, as long as you worship and attend a church. He knows that we are not perfect.

Not everybody thinks that way. They believe that church membership is a matter of obedience, not a matter of preference. A church should have the right doctrine, the right practices, and traditions. The people of the church should be sober-minded and give no offence because of the way they dress or behave. We should keep the old traditions as much as possible. After all, the Bible does not change either.

How do we respond to these differences of opinion? Questions and Answers 54–56 of the Heidelberg Catechism deal with these issues in accordance with God's Word, and not in accordance with our own thoughts and opinions. They examine these issues based on the Word of God. God always has the final answer. In this chapter, I discuss what it means to be a member of God's church.

Scripture

1 Corinthians 12:12–25

One Body with Many Members

12 For just as the body is one and has many members, and all the members of the body, though many, are one body, so it is with Christ.

13 For in one Spirit we were all baptized into one body—Jews or Greeks, slaves or free—and all were made to drink of one Spirit.

14 For the body does not consist of one member but of many.

15 If the foot should say, "Because I am not a hand, I do not belong to the body," that would not make it any less a part of the body.

16 And if the ear should say, "Because I am not an eye, I do not belong to the body," that would not make it any less a part of the body.

17 If the whole body were an eye, where would be the sense of hearing? If the whole body were an ear, where would be the sense of smell?

18 But as it is, God arranged the members in the body, each one of them, as he chose.

19 If all were a single member, where would the body be?

20 As it is, there are many parts, yet one body.

21 The eye cannot say to the hand, "I have no need of you," nor again the head to the feet, "I have no need of you."

22 On the contrary, the parts of the body that seem to be weaker are indispensable,

23 and on those parts of the body that we think less honorable we bestow the greater honor, and our unpresentable parts are treated with greater modesty,

24 which our more presentable parts do not require. But God has so composed the body, giving greater honor to the part that lacked it,

25 that there may be no division in the body, but that the members may have the same care for one another.

The Apostles' Creed

This creed is called the Apostles' Creed, not because it was written by the apostles themselves, but because it contains a brief summary of their teachings. It sets forth their doctrine, as has been said by Philip Schaff, "in sublime simplicity, in unsurpassable brevity, in the most beautiful order, and with liturgical solemnity." The Apostles' Creed is based on the creed used in Rome around AD 400, which in turn goes back another two hundred years. It is typical of the creeds used in the western part of the Roman Empire.

I.   1. I believe in God the Father almighty,
Creator of heaven and earth.

II.   2. I believe in Jesus Christ,
his only-begotten Son, our Lord;

3. he was conceived by the Holy Spirit,
born of the virgin Mary;

4. suffered under Pontius Pilate,
was crucified, dead, and buried;
he descended into hell.

5. On the third day he arose from the dead;

6. he ascended into heaven,
and sits at the right hand
of God the Father almighty;

7. from there he will come to judge
the living and the dead.

III.   8. I believe in the Holy Spirit;

9. I believe a holy catholic Christian church,
the communion of saints;

10. the forgiveness of sins;

11. the resurrection of the body;

12. and the life everlasting. Amen.

Heidelberg Catechism

54. Q. What do you believe
concerning the *holy catholic Christian church?*

A. I believe that the Son of God,[1]
out of the whole human race,[2]
from the beginning of the world to its end,[3]
gathers, defends, and preserves for himself, [4]
by his Spirit and Word,[5]
in the unity of the true faith,[6]
a church chosen to everlasting life.[7]

And I believe that I am[8]
and forever shall remain
a living member of it.[9]

[1] Jn 10:11; Acts 20:28; Eph 4:11–13; Col 1:18.
[2] Gen 26:4; Rev 5:9.
[3] Is 59:21; 1 Cor 11:26.
[4] Ps 129:1–5; Mt 16:18; Jn 10:28–30.
[5] Rom 1:16; 10:14–17; Eph 5:26.
[6] Acts 2:42–47; Eph 4:1–6.
[7] Rom 8:29; Eph 1:3–14.
[8] 1 Jn 3:14, 19–21.
[9] Ps 23:6; Jn 10:27, 28; 1 Cor 1:4–9; 1 Pet 1:3–5.

55. Q. What do you understand by
         the communion of saints?

     A. First,
         that believers, all and everyone,
         as members of Christ
         have communion with him
         and share in all his treasures and gifts.[1]

         Second,
         that everyone is duty-bound
         to use his gifts
         readily and cheerfully
         for the benefit and well-being
         of the other members.[2]

     [1] Rom 8:32; 1 Cor 6:17; 12:4-7, 12, 13; 1 Jn 1:3.
     [2] Rom 12:4-8; 1 Cor 12:20-27; 13:1-7; Phil 2:4-8.

56. Q. What do you believe
         concerning *the forgiveness of sins*?

     A. I believe that God,
         because of Christ's satisfaction,
         will no more remember
         my sins,[1]
         nor my sinful nature,
         against which I have to struggle
         all my life,[2]
         but will graciously grant me
         the righteousness of Christ,
         that I may never come into condemnation.[3]

     [1] Ps 103:3, 4, 10, 12; Mic 7:18, 19; 2 Cor 5:18-21; 1 Jn 1:7; 2:2.
     [2] Rom 7:21-25.
     [3] Jn 3:17, 18; 5:24; Rom 8:1, 2.

A Holy Church

The catechism asks, "What do you believe concerning *the holy catholic Christian church*?" The words in italics are from the Apostles' Creed. This creed is one of the earliest and most widely accepted statements of Christian faith and continues to be a fundamental statement of Christian faith in many denominations, including Roman Catholic, Eastern Orthodox, Anglican, Lutheran, Reformed, and many Protestant churches.

Nevertheless, these various denominations may not always share a common understanding of these statements. Therefore, it is crucial to examine the biblical perspective on the concept of the church.

The word *church* is borrowed from the Greek word *kuriakon*, meaning "of the Lord" or "belonging to the Lord." Over time, the word has been used to denote both the physical building, made up of bricks and mortar, of bamboo and lashed rope, and the religious community itself.

The Apostles' Creed has in mind the latter usage, referring to the spiritual church, which exists of living stones and living members. That church is called a *holy* church, and therefore, the members are holy members. That doesn't imply a group of excessively devout individuals. Contrary to such assumptions, Christians who attend church are just as prone to sin as anyone else.

Committed Christians, however, do not want to live in their sins. They are sorry for their sins and daily ask for forgiveness. They also try to live according to God's laws. Because of that, the Holy Spirit makes them holy. That is why, in the catechism, the doctrine concerning the church is dealt with under the heading of the Holy Spirit. It is God the Holy Spirit who makes the church on earth holy.

It is important to properly understand this. Many people, both inside and outside the church, find all kinds of things wrong with the church by looking at certain members of the church and finding them wanting. They observe that they fall into many of the same sins as they themselves do. For example, they are not always as kind to their neighbour as they should be. They can be judgmental. They can be hard to get along with. They can be harsh, and sometimes even dishonest in their business dealings. And so the list can go on.

It is no wonder that those who do not belong to a church will say, "If that is what the people of the church are like, then I want nothing to do with them. They are all a bunch of hypocrites."

What is their mistake? Well, they look at people. They look at the people and, from there, determine what the church of God is like.

It is understandable that secular people do that, for they only go by what they see and experience. But is that also what we, as Christians, should do? Of course, it is true, as the Bible also teaches, that the way in which the members of the church ought to conduct themselves is very important. But that is not where we begin. We do not begin with man but with God. That is also what the Heidelberg Catechism does.

God's Work

Firstly, it's essential to recognize that the church is the work of the triune God. Accordingly, the Apostles' Creed is divided into three parts: God the Father and our creation, God the Son and our redemption, and God the Holy Spirit and our sanctification.

The catechism, in its distinct sections, explains what this triune God has accomplished and will continue to do. It guides us in understanding how we should place our faith *in* him. This reflection is mirrored in the language of the Apostles' Creed, where we affirm our belief *in* God the Father, *in* God the Son, and *in* God the Holy Spirit. Our trust is solely *in* this triune God—we believe in him and no one else.

However, then there is a shift in focus. It no longer addresses what we believe *in*, but rather *what* we believe. This shift is evident in the wording of the Apostles' Creed. While we declare that we believe in the Holy Spirit, we now confess that we believe *a* holy catholic Christian church, the communion of saints, and the forgiveness of sins. We are not stating that we believe *in* these things. Instead, we believe them because God has revealed them to us.

And so, here we deal with the *content* of our faith, not in *whom* we believe, but *what* we believe. If you want to know what the church of God ought to look like, then you must go to God's Word. And then you have to look at whether or not the church has the characteristics that God attributes to her in his Word. If those characteristics are not there, then you are not speaking about the church of God.

Thus, we must be very careful how we see and speak about the church of God. We must look at it, not from a human perspective, not from what we expect from the church, but what God expects from each of us.

This is very well spelled out in question and answer 54 of the Heidelberg Catechism. It first says that the Son of God gathers his church out of the whole human race. That, then, is one of the important characteristics of the church. The Lord gathers his church from every nation and tribe.

For that reason, we speak about the *catholic* church. The word *catholic* comes from the Greek word *katholikos*, meaning "universal." Although the term is most commonly associated with the Roman Catholic Church, it actually applies to those churches all over the world that faithfully reflect biblical characteristics. The Lord gathers his church from all over the world and puts all peoples on equal footing.

That is clear from the Bible. Even in the Old Testament, the Lord God added people from various nations to his church. Think about Rahab the harlot, for example. Or about Ruth the Moabitess. Both of these women are even mentioned in the genealogy of the Lord Jesus Christ himself. Yet, both these women came from foreign nations. They spoke a different language, had different customs, and came from different cultures.

God does not discriminate. He does not elevate one nation above another. He does not state either that one skin colour is more desirable than another. He does not say that Blacks are inferior to Whites or vice versa. Nor does he say that the American Indian is inferior to the White man. No, God gathers his church from all tribes and nations. He gathers them from the Africans, the Chinese, the Japanese, the Koreans, the Russians, etc.

He does not state either that one culture is superior to another. No, the Lord is indiscriminate in the way that he chooses his people. He makes no distinctions.

To be sure, that includes more than just the colour of our skin or the language that we speak. People are different in other ways. People have different temperaments, different gifts, and different abilities. Each person has their own weaknesses or strengths. We are all unique. We all have our own characteristics. Each person also has their own background which makes them the kind of person that they are. Despite these differences, God chooses all kinds of people. He does not favour one over the other. No, we are not any different in his sight. He chooses us unconditionally.

Therefore, we, too, must see the church in the same way. We may not accept or reject others because of outward appearances, or other characteristics. By nature, we like those people who are most like us. We like those who speak the same kind of language, who have the same customs, the same culture, and the same way of doing things. We are not attracted to people we consider to be poor, or to be ugly, or who smell different from us. We do not like people who are on the fringe of society. We do not like drug addicts, sex workers, or alcoholics. We do not like people who are loud and who draw attention to themselves. We do not like people who do not think exactly like we do.

We aren't inherently inclined towards any of these individuals, and that's understandable, since it requires compassion and understanding. Cultivating a habit of self-reflection is crucial, prompting us to contemplate our own weaknesses and quirks. Recalling our past experiences helps us recognize instances where we may have unfairly judged or mistreated others. This demands humility and effort, but it's essential. We should refrain from assessing others solely based on our personal preferences and aversions.

You may ask, "What about the way people conduct themselves? Does God not say that he loves those who do his will?" For example, we read in Exodus 19:5, "Now if you obey me fully and keep my covenant, then out of all nations you will be my treasured possession. Although the whole earth is mine" (NIV84).

But it's crucial to understand that the covenant between God and his children isn't contingent on our good behaviour. On the contrary, it's established despite our bad behaviour. Christians are sinners, and that is why they need the Lord Jesus to rescue them from the horrible consequences of sin. By emptying himself of all the glory and riches he had in heaven (Philippians. 2:5–8), the Lord Jesus came to earth to restore our relationship with God. By being perfect in his conduct and speech, and by bearing the wrath of God against sin, he actively and passively fulfilled the law for us. Through faith in him, his perfect obedience was credited to us.

Answer 55 of the catechism tells us that we "share in Christ and all his treasures and gifts." Do you know what one of the greatest gifts is that we receive from the Lord our God? It is the forgiveness of sins. And that is so beautifully stated in answer 56. There, it states, "I believe that God will no more remember my sins, nor my sinful nature." That bears repeating: he will no more remember my sins. He will also overlook my shortcomings and my weaknesses. He will not hold my sinful nature against me. He will treat me like his own son who was obedient in every respect to the law. What a wonderful confession!

Struggles

Oh sure, life is full of struggles. The catechism also states that, for it speaks about the sinful nature against which I have to struggle all my life. There must be that constant battle against our sinful inclinations. But it is a struggle within the covenant that God has established. It is not a struggle that we fight in our own strength.

Each individual faces their own struggle in this regard. As mentioned previously, each person is distinct, having their own set of challenges to navigate. Every individual faces their own struggle in this regard. There are those who are born with certain sinful inclinations that others do not have. There are those who are born with certain weaknesses.

Think of those who are born with developmental disabilities.

There are also those who have greater difficulty controlling their tempers than others. And there are those who come from dysfunctional or broken homes, and who, because of their background, have difficulty getting along with others. They have all kinds of emotional baggage. There are those who have been abused as children, and whose adult lives are seriously affected by it. There are those who have been taught wrong habits as a child, and who have difficulty breaking those wrong habits.

All these people, with their various backgrounds and challenges, must struggle against their sins all their lives. What poses a challenge for one may not be so for another. Nonetheless, each person must confront their own sins. Thankfully, the Lord God comprehends our struggles, and likewise, we should extend understanding to one another in this regard.

Therefore, we do not judge as the world does. We judge as God does. And God loves all those who, despite their background and difficult circumstances, trust in him alone. He loves those who hate their sin, and who flee to him for deliverance. For he promises to all those who believe and who struggle against their sins every day of their lives that they will be saved. They are the ones who belong to his church. For the Lord our God is a compassionate God. He is much more compassionate than any of us. There is no comparison. And yet, we must also strive to be like him in that regard.

The catechism also says that he "gathers his church from the beginning of the world to its end." That is also very comforting to know. The church began with Adam and Eve. Despite their terrible fall into sin, the Lord God still looked favourably upon them. They still received God's grace. And so it has been throughout the ages. The Lord God built his church also from a man such as Jacob, who cheated and lied in order to get his birthright. God built this church through a man like Judah, who visited harlots. He gathered his church through a man like David, who committed adultery and who was a murderer. All of these men sinned against God, but they went to him for the forgiveness of sins.

And look at what is said about the church in the New Testament. Think of the church in Corinth, for example. There was a lot wrong with that congregation. There were those who engaged in sexual immorality, who sued their fellow believers in court, who became drunk, who ate meat offered to idols, and who ignored the poor, and thus offended other church members.

And yet, the Holy Spirit still addresses those people as the church of the Lord Jesus Christ. Why? Only because of God's great love. They struggled with their sins. They sought their salvation in the Lord and Saviour Jesus Christ. They believed. The apostle Paul taught them about their sins, and they repented and asked the Lord for forgiveness. Hence they showed themselves to be members of the church of the Lord Jesus Christ, God's people.

The catechism also says that he gathers, defends, and preserves for himself "a church chosen to everlasting life." God's church is the elect church. Note well that also here Christ is in the center. The church belongs to him. He gathers her for himself. He does that in the first place for his own sake, to bring glory to his name.

He does not just choose loose, disconnected individuals. No, he chooses and gathers a church, made up of all kinds of people, to everlasting life. God is, first of all, concerned with his flock, his sheep. He is the one who brings them together. And together, they are God's elect. As believers, you and I are meant to experience eternal life.

Unity

Another characteristic of the church is that the Lord Jesus Christ gathers his church in the unity of true faith. The unity of the church is first of all unity with Christ, and also unity with one another. That's why we seek each other and hold on to each other. In so doing, we bear with each other's shortcomings and idiosyncrasies. What does that mean? What does such unity imply? Some people think that unity implies uniformity, that it means that we must all think the same and do the same.

That's wrong. Unity does not imply that we must agree on everything or be alike in everything. As long as there is a church here on earth, there will always be differences of opinion. Because of our sin, we cannot avoid that. True unity will happen only in the life hereafter.

For the church of today, however, it means that she must want to submit herself to the Word of God. It means that we, as members of God's church, do not want our differences to remain. It means that we do everything in our power to understand what God has to say to us.

For the catechism says further that he gathers his church by his Spirit and Word. Those are the means by which he gathers his church. Note well, that the catechism does not mention the office bearers, the ministers, the elders, or the deacons. No, the catechism speaks about God's Spirit and Word. Those are ultimately the means that God uses. Everything else is subordinate to his Spirit and his Word. For, once again, it is God's work in the first place. That is where we must put our emphasis.

For that reason, church membership is important. We should want to belong to a church that is faithful to God's Word, acknowledges that God is sovereign and has the final answer for all things. A true church must have a burning desire to please God at all costs. The church must be an instrument of the Holy Spirit.

At Pentecost the Holy Spirit was poured out upon the church. The Holy Spirit then moved the apostle Peter to give his wonderful Pentecostal address. He spoke, and thousands came to faith. Peter was merely an instrument in the hand of the Holy Spirit. And so it is also with the office bearers. They are mere mouthpieces of God. God is at work, not humans. It was the Holy Spirit who drove the apostles to the outlying areas of the world. It was the Holy Spirit who worked in the heart of the apostle Paul so that he could become converted and become an ambassador of the Lord Jesus Christ. God gathers his church, not humans. He does so by his Spirit and his Word.

Our Response

Many churches today no longer regard unity as a fundamental trait of the church. They maintain that different churches can coexist independently, with little to no interaction, while still professing unity. They argue that God is the One who binds us together, uniting us through faith, and adopt the fantasy of the "invisible church." God's church is not invisible. The inspired authors of the Bible did not write to invisible gatherings of God's people all over the world.

They make the mistake and go to the other extreme and only look at what God does. They do not look at our responsibility. For we must consider both. God does his work, but we must also respond. God does indeed give us a role to play.

One of the characteristics of the church is that she is one in faith. The Lord God makes us brothers and sisters in the Lord. That means that we must also act as brothers and sisters in the

Lord. Brothers and sisters in the Lord care for one another. They share meals together. They have communion with one another. In fact, that is also why we are so keen on seeking unity with other churches. We see this as a command from God. We do not want to remain apart from others. For that is a sin.

Therefore, question and answer 55 is also so important. There, the question is asked, "What do you understand *by the communion of saints*?" The answer begins by speaking about our unity with Christ. It says that believers have communion with him and share in all his treasures and gifts. Indeed, our unity is, first of all, in Christ.

We share all his treasures and gifts. What are those treasures and gifts? They are especially the forgiveness of sins and eternal life. Those treasures are all the gifts of the Holy Spirit. They also include God's Word, and the office bearers who administer God's Word. Those treasures and gifts are the fruit of the Holy Spirit, such as love, kindness, compassion, peace, and wisdom. And there are many more. The gifts of God to the church are numerous.

But now the second part of this answer states that we are duty bound also to share those gifts with others. With whom exactly? Who are those others? Well, we must share them and use them for the benefit and well-being of the other members of the church. In other words, we may not keep them for ourselves. No, we must share them with everyone. We must share them with everyone whom we know to be our brothers and sisters in the Lord.

We are told in 1 Corinthians 12 that the church is the body of Christ. A body has many parts, and although each part has a different function, they belong together.

To be sure, we also have to use those gifts outside of the church. That is also very, very important. But they must first be used in the church. As Galatians 6:10 reveals, "Therefore, as we have opportunity, let us do good to all people, especially to those who belong to the family of believers" (NIV84).

And so, we have to help one another. How? Well, let us first look at one of the most important gifts given to the church, namely the forgiveness of sins. We confess in question and answer 56 that God graciously forgives me my sins and grants me the righteousness of Christ so that I may never come into condemnation. Isn't that wonderful? We do not stand condemned before God.

But what about each other? Do we do that with one another, within our own church? Are you able to forgive others their sins and shortcomings? Or do you harbour hatred and resentment against some of our brothers and sisters in the Lord? Are you unable to bear other's differences? Do you stand in judgment over others because they are different from you or because they act differently from you? Do you play favourites?

Well, if that is the case, then you are not reflecting what God says in his Word about the members of the church. For, let's remember that we believe a holy catholic church, and that we believe the forgiveness of sins. We believe them because of the way that God describes them in his Word. He tells us what his church *is* like and *must be* like. He tells us what the forgiveness of sins is all about and how we, too, must practice it.

If God's view of the church and our view of the church are at odds with each other, then there is something seriously wrong. If the church does not try in every respect to do that which God requires of her, then in the long run she will cease to be a church. For in the end, she will no longer reflect what a church ought to look like.

And the same thing is true of the members of the church. If they are not able to forgive others their sins and shortcomings, then, if they persist in this, they will, in the end, cease to be Christians. Satan will take hold of them.

The same thing is true of our unity with other Christians. Often, unity does not come about, because we are not able to forgive one another. We remember the things that have been said and done to us. We are suspicious of one another. But the Lord God, who forgives our sins and shortcomings, also commands us to forgive others. That is what it means to be one together. That is what it means to belong to Christ. That is what it means to belong to God's church.

In the church, God is at work. He is the one who gathers, defends, and preserves his church. Some of the old church fathers would sometimes refer to the church as the ark of God. They spoke in that way about the church because, like the ark during the flood, those who were inside of it would be safe. The floods would come, and the storms would rage, and all kinds of dangers would lurk outside. But inside that ark, God's people would find a safe haven.

That is the way it is with the church. The Lord God is the one who gathers the church. He is at work in us. And he is Almighty God. And therefore, we do not have to be afraid.

It is a wonderful thing to belong to God's church. That is where God is at work, in us and through us. That is where you will find the forgiveness of sins. That is where you'll find a people to be caring for one another because of the treasures and gifts that God has given them. It is only in the church where you'll find such riches. *He* is the one who gathers his church. It is his work alone.

Reflection

1. Take a moment to think about the fact that you're in front of a God who judges you without any unfair prejudice or selfish bias. How does this change how you see other people and how you treat them?

2. Have you embraced the fact that you are just as great a sinner as others and that you are saved by grace alone? How does that view of sin and grace impact the way that you view the church of God?

Chapter 8
Seeing Others as God Sees Us

*"He has removed our sins as far from us
as the east is from the west."*
Psalm 103:12 (NLT)

*"Forgiveness is not an occasional act;
it is a permanent attitude."*
Martin Luther King Jr.

*"Forgiveness is the key that unlocks the door of
resentment and the handcuffs of hate.
It is the power that breaks the chains of bitterness
and the shackles of selfishness."*
Corrie ten Boom

Introduction

Although the concept of forgiveness of sins is an important tenet in many religious and philosophical traditions, Christianity is unique because it emphasizes that forgiveness is not primarily a human activity but a divine one. Complete forgiveness can only be found through faith in Jesus Christ who vicariously died on the cross, being forsaken by God and man. Forgiveness is a divine act of grace, extended to humanity through God's mercy, rather than something earned through individual merit.

True forgiveness is found only with God, who reconciles himself to us and to each other by removing all the barriers that exist between us. For human beings to forgive others is very difficult. It is our nature to hang on to past wrongs and to live with resentments and desires to seek revenge. Only in God can you overcome that.

In this chapter, we encounter a woman, a known sinner, whose life takes a profound turn because of her encounter with the Lord Jesus Christ, who forgives her sins. Her transformation is clear from the intense gratitude and immense joy she expresses, signalling a significant shift in her relationship with God and her neighbour.

Scripture

Luke 7:36–50

Jesus Anointed by a Sinful Woman

36 One of the Pharisees asked him to eat with him, and he went into the Pharisee's house and reclined at table.

37 And behold, a woman of the city, who was a sinner, when she learned that he was reclining at table in the Pharisee's house, brought an alabaster flask of ointment,

38 and standing behind him at his feet, weeping, she began to wet his feet with her tears and wiped them with the hair of her head and kissed his feet and anointed them with the ointment.

39 Now when the Pharisee who had invited him saw this, he said to himself, "If this man were a prophet, he would have known who and what sort of woman this is who is touching him, for she is a sinner."

40 And Jesus answering said to him, "Simon, I have something to say to you." And he answered, "Say it, Teacher."

41 "A certain moneylender had two debtors. One owed five hundred denarii, and the other fifty.

42 When they could not pay, he cancelled the debt of both. Now which of them will love him more?"

43 Simon answered, "The one, I suppose, for whom he cancelled the larger debt." And he said to him, "You have judged rightly."

44 Then turning toward the woman he said to Simon, "Do you see this woman? I entered your house; you gave me no water for my feet, but she has wet my feet with her tears and wiped them with her hair.

45 You gave me no kiss, but from the time I came in she has not ceased to kiss my feet.

46 You did not anoint my head with oil, but she has anointed my feet with ointment.

47 Therefore I tell you, her sins, which are many, are forgiven—for she loved much. But he who is forgiven little, loves little."

48 And he said to her, "Your sins are forgiven."

49 Then those who were at table with him began to say among themselves, "Who is this, who even forgives sins?"

50 And he said to the woman, "Your faith has saved you; go in peace."

Heidelberg Catechism

126. Q. What is the fifth petition (of the Lord's Prayer)?

   A. *And forgive us our debts,*
      as we also have forgiven our debtors.

   That is:
   For the sake of Christ's blood,
   do not impute to us,
   wretched sinners,
   any of our transgressions,
   nor the evil which still clings to us,[1]
   as we also find this evidence of your grace in us
   that we are fully determined
   wholeheartedly to forgive our neighbour.[2]

[1] Ps 51:1–7; 143:2; Rom 8:1; 1 Jn 2:1, 2.
[2] Mt 6:14, 15; 18:21–35.

Open Your Eyes

"Simon, do you see this woman?" That's the question Jesus asks in Luke 7:44. Why does he ask it? It seems like an odd question. It was clear that Simon had seen her. That is evident from the account that we just read. She came into Simon's house uninvited while they were eating. Simon the Pharisee was quite perturbed. He did not like that intrusion.

He was also irritated with Jesus for not telling her off and for not right away getting rid of her. She had no reason to be there. She was disruptive and, to make matters even worse, she was well known in the town where Simon lived and had a bad reputation.

The passage in Luke indicates that she was a well-known sinner. Since sexual immorality is usually seen as the worst kind of sin, one could easily conclude that she was a sex worker. But the text does not tell us exactly what her sinful life was. It could also be that she was a common thief. Whatever it was, Simon knew all about this woman. As far as Simon was concerned, Jesus is the one who should be more observant. He should know with whom he is dealing.

Jesus fully understands that Simon is keenly aware of the woman's presence. Indeed, all eyes are on her as she enters the house and stands behind Jesus. Everyone is staring at her and painfully aware of her unwelcome presence. Why does Jesus now say to Simon that he must see this woman? What exactly does the Lord Jesus want Simon to see?

Well, Jesus wants Simon to look at her much differently than he is doing now. He does not want him to see her as everybody else sees her: as a reject, an embarrassment, someone the world would be better off without, a hopeless sinner. No, Jesus wants Simon to see the woman for who she truly is. He wants him to see that woman in a completely different light. Simon must open his eyes and see her, not in her relationship to man, but in her relationship to God. Jesus wants him to see her through the eyes of God.

But that perceptual shift is a big problem not only for Simon, but for all of us. To be able to do that, we must open our eyes to our own sins and to how God sees us. The only way to do that is first to observe others compassionately and without bias, second to be keenly aware of our own sins and shortcomings, and finally to forgive like Jesus.

Being Kind to Others

Luke 7 does not explain why Simon the Pharisee invited Jesus to dinner with him. He did not do that because he wanted to honour him, or because he was favourably inclined to him, for he did not treat him in the way that you would typically treat a guest.

It was the custom in those days that when guests were invited to someone's home, one of the servants would wash their feet, or, at the very least, make water available for the guests' feet. The visitors' feet would be caked with dirt and dust after walking in sandals on dusty roads.

After washing their feet, the host would typically welcome each guest and greet them with a kiss to make them feel welcome and to let them know they were honoured guests.

Anointing the guests' heads with some olive oil was also a courtesy. No one is sure exactly why this was done, but it was probably done to give some relief from the hot oriental sun. It was done out of respect.

Simon did not do any of these things for Jesus. He was not interested in honouring him. He was only curious. He wanted to find out more about the man Jesus.

Simon was a Pharisee. As such, he belonged to a privileged and highly regarded class of people. Pharisees were well educated and were in a position of leadership and authority. Even the Romans in many ways deferred to them. Hence Pharisees were highly regarded by all. They were in a singular class.

The Pharisees also saw themselves as deserving to be so highly regarded. After all, they were the epitome of piety. As learned men, they knew the Scriptures thoroughly and kept the laws meticulously. They considered themselves to be examples of propriety, discernment, and wisdom. For that reason, they did not associate on the same level with others they considered inferior to them. They certainly did not associate with sinful women.

Thus it was a shock for this woman to do what she did. She entered Simon's house uninvited. That in itself was not unusual.

From what we know about the customs of those days, people could enter the open court of a home where a dinner was given. They would not seat themselves among the guests but along the wall. From there they could observe everything and even engage in conversation with the people present.

But it was unusual that this woman entered the premises of a strict Pharisee. Pharisees were quite condescending to women, especially women with bad reputations. They did not make such people feel welcome or appreciated. They shunned them and made them feel unwelcome. Nevertheless, she entered Simon's home and even found the courage to approach Jesus and stand at his feet.

Now, just picture this. In those days, people did not sit on a chair like we do today. Instead, they would recline on low couches arranged around a low table. Each person would face the table, lying slantwise, with their feet stretched out behind them. They would lean on their left arm to free their right hand to handle the food. And so the woman would be standing behind Jesus, who was reclining at the table; that is, she would be behind his extended feet.

Then something remarkable happens. She is overwhelmed with emotion as she stands behind him and begins to weep. Luther says that the tears were "heart water." Hers were genuine.

The tears drip onto the feet of the Lord Jesus. She did not expect to have that kind of emotional outburst at that time. She did not want this to happen. But she could not help herself.

When she sees what she has done, she loosens her hair and, with it, wipes the feet of the Lord Jesus clean. Then she even pours perfume on his feet.

She had taken that expensive perfume along because she had intended to anoint the head of Jesus. In this way, she wanted to show her thankfulness to him. But then, instead, she not only anoints his feet, but also kisses them, not just once but repeatedly. And Jesus allows her to do that.

This is too much for Simon. He does not voice his objections out loud. No, he keeps his thoughts to himself, thinking that if Jesus knew who this woman was, he would not have allowed her to touch him. He thinks, "How can this man call himself a prophet? A true prophet would've known better."

However, Jesus knows exactly what Simon is thinking. Thereby he proves himself to be a true prophet. Except Simon is too blind to realize this. But, so that the eyes of this Pharisee could be opened, he does not directly confront him but instead tells him a parable.

He tells him the story of two men who owed money to a certain moneylender. The one owed five hundred denarii and the other fifty. Both amounts are quite large. A denarius represented about a day's wages. However, the one owed ten times as much as the other.

Jesus says neither of them had money to pay back their debt, so the moneylender cancelled the debt of both. Then Jesus asks Simon, "Now which of them will love him more?" In other words, "Who do you think would be the most thankful?" Simon knows what answer he is expected to give, for it is obvious. It would be the one who had the greatest debt forgiven.

Now Jesus has Simon exactly where he wants him. Therefore, now he says, "Simon, do you see this woman?" Up to this point, all that Simon saw was a sinful woman. He saw her in accordance with the reputation that she had. He saw her as someone who is inferior to him. He saw her as an intruder, as a worthless human being.

But that is not how Jesus saw her. On the contrary, he says

in verse 47 that this woman is someone whose many sins are forgiven. Consequently, she is someone who is acceptable in the sight of God. God loves her in spite of who she is.

Jesus wants Simon to see her in the same way. He wants Simon to go outside of himself. He does not want him to think about the reputation that she previously had, or what the other Pharisees think about her, or what the townspeople think of her. No, he wants Simon to see the woman for who she truly is.

In fact, he is saying, "She stood there weeping, Simon. Why would that be? Think about it. Look further. Those tears well up from her heart. They well up because she realizes what a sinful woman she was and still is. Oh yes, her sins were many, but all her sins have been forgiven. That is why she wept, Simon. These are tears of joy."

"You, on the other hand, Simon, think that your sins are few and that your good works outweigh your bad works, and that for that reason, there is no great need for you to have the forgiveness of sins. But, think again. You too are a great sinner in need of the forgiveness of sins."

How often do we not look at people in the way that Simon the Pharisee does? We look at certain people in the church, as well as outside of the church, and we remember them by their reputation. We remember the kinds of things they have done in the past. And we keep on judging them for it. We see them as inferior, as damaged goods.

Or we see people who socially do not function as well as others. They have difficulty sometimes keeping their emotions in check in public. They become easily angry or pout, saying and doing foolish and sometimes rude things that make others uncomfortable. Or we see people who have difficulties in their family life and who have all kinds of personal problems. Or we see people with mental or physical disabilities and judge them as inferior. Frequently, we even do that within our own families.

But think to yourself, "What does the Lord Jesus see? Does he judge in the same way?" He doesn't, does he?

There are reasons why people do certain things and act in a certain way. Often it is because of bad experiences in the past, especially during childhood. They have been hurt. They are damaged goods and are different because of it. They feel the judgment that they receive from others. And it grieves them. They don't know what to do about it. They don't know how to change their behaviour. They are full of guilt. They often feel that God is angry with them because of their sins.

No doubt, that is also how it was with that woman who entered Simon's house. It is likely that Jesus had contact with this woman at some time and told her that her sins have been forgiven. That took a tremendous weight off her shoulders. After that, she no longer felt divine disapproval. She no longer felt that God was angry with her. The Lord Jesus, by telling her that her sins have been forgiven, puts her into a new relationship with God. No wonder she was so joyful.

The catechism says that we must see the evidence of God's grace in us and that we wholeheartedly forgive our neighbours. When you wholeheartedly forgive others their sins, you no longer look upon them because of their sins. That means you no longer act according to the person's reputation. When you forgive someone their sins, you do not do that just once or twice; you do that 7 x 70 times (Matthew 18:22). In other words, you forgive so often that the process is habitual, and you no longer have to number the times. There is no end to it.

Consequently, we should all look carefully at other people. Young people as well. Perhaps there's someone in your class who is a bit different. Such children may not be as nice as some other kids. They draw attention to themselves in strange ways and sometimes make a nuisance of themselves. How do you treat them? Like rejects?

But ask yourself, is that what the Lord Jesus wants you to do? Think about how he treated those who are different. He treated everyone with kindness and love. He did not look at them because of their sins, or their disabilities, but because of the loving relationship that he has established with them and because every human being is created in the image of God. That includes others from different races and colours and nationalities, and even different religions. We must see them with the compassionate eyes of Jesus. That is also how we should look at our neighbour and every person God places on our path—even our enemies. However, the only way you can do that is if you first examine yourself and see your own sins.

Self-Examination

We read in Psalm 139:23–24, "Search me, O God, and know my heart! Try me and know my thoughts! And see if there be any grievous way in me and lead me in the way everlasting!"

That sinful woman in the passage had been keenly aware of her sinful state. She allowed God to search her heart and saw how she departed from God's ways. And she knew what other people said about her and what they thought about her. These things grieved her.

How can I be so sure of that? Well, otherwise she would not have reacted to the Lord Jesus in the way she did. And she would not have had the audacity to go up to him in the midst of high society and weep her eyes out in front of them because of how she felt about what Jesus had done for her. For Jesus had told her that all her sins are forgiven. At that point, the weight of her sins was lifted from her shoulders, and now she is full of joy. She is tremendously relieved. She is unspeakably thankful.

Is that also how you feel? The catechism says that if we pray for the forgiveness of our sins, then we pray to the Lord our God that "for the sake of Christ's blood, do not impute to us, wretched sinners, any of our transgressions, nor the evil which still clings to us."

The only way that you can pray such a petition is if you have some sense of your own sinfulness; if you have some understanding of how you sin against God every day, indeed every moment of each day; if you have some sense of how you wrong others, in your attitude, in the way that you treat them, in the way that you think about them. You must have some sense of the great debt you owe God.

The more you realize the enormous debt you owe, the more thankful you will be. The more you will love the One who has cancelled your debts and forgiven you your sins. In other words, the more that you will love the Lord Jesus.

Simon the Pharisee did not have a sense of his own sins. He saw himself as an upstanding citizen of God's kingdom. He thought that God was lucky to have him as one of his servants: "Look at how good I am, oh God." And that is why he judged others as severely as he did. He was arrogant.

Sometimes, people stop going to church because of the sinful people they find there. They go to another church where they are more appreciated. To a church where they feel most comfortable.

Or they stop going to church altogether.

The problem is that we tend to elevate ourselves and to lower others, to bring them down. That's what you and I are like in accordance with our sinful nature.

But we may not give in to that. We must fight that. Our confessions, which are based on the Bible, do not allow us to do that either. The catechism is a very personal confession. It speaks about us as wretched and miserable sinners, and about our sins, and about the evil which still clings to us. Jesus says in Matthew 7:5, "Look at yourself first. Take out the log from your own eye before you take out the splinter of your neighbour's eye." Only then will you be able to forgive the sins of others.

Forgive Like Jesus

To forgive is not easy. Someone may have really hurt us in the past, and some continue to do that. It isn't easy to forgive those people. And yet, that is what God requires. For note well that Jesus ties the forgiveness of our sins to the forgiveness we extend to others. Those two must go hand in hand. Unless we forgive those who have sinned against us, and who have harmed us, God will not forgive us.

Not that the forgiveness of our sins depends on the forgiveness we give to others. We do not receive the forgiveness of sins because of anything we have done. No, it is a result of what God has done. And then, if we are truly thankful that God forgives us our sins, we cannot help but forgive others. Through his forgiveness, he makes us new creatures and creates in us an attitude, a predisposition for forgiveness.

His forgiveness gives us a heart of compassion. If that is not there, then something is seriously wrong with you or me spiritually.

God's forgiveness of our sins must always result in the forgiveness of the sins of others. There is no other way.

Yet, many people still have difficulty with this. They look at the damage that has been done and at the incredible pain that has been inflicted, and that continues to be inflicted. And so they think forgiveness does not take the harm of sin seriously enough.

Please note, however, that God *does* take sin very seriously. The forgiveness of sins is never meant to excuse the sinner. It doesn't say, "It is all right for you to hurt others, and to continue to do that."

No! But God wants you to put it all into a proper perspective. Consider what God has done for us through our Lord and Saviour Jesus Christ. Jesus Christ is the proof that God did not just pass over our sins as if they are not a big deal.

For what did Jesus do? He paid the penalty for our sins. That did not come cheap. He had to shed his blood. He had to give his life. He had to suffer the agony of hell, being forsaken by God and by humanity.

And so, don't think that now anyone is scot-free, including those who have sinned against us and have done serious damage. No, sin has consequences for everyone.

Sometimes those consequences are experienced in this life. If you are a sexual abuser, a thief or liar, or a perpetual drunk, then you will most likely receive some form of punishment in one way or the other already in this life.

But ultimately, those who do not repent from their sins, will experience the eternal wrath of God in the life hereafter. There is no worse outcome than that.

And so we may commiserate that in this life those who sin against us do not receive their just judgment. Indeed. But then remember what the Lord your God says, "Do not take revenge, my friends, but leave room for God's wrath, for it is written: 'It is mine to avenge; I will repay'" (Romans 12:19).

That is the fate of those who do not repent.

But what about us who believe?

Well, for us, he has visited his wrath on his dearly beloved Son and through him, he forgives us our sins. That was the greatest act of love ever shown here on earth. God did not want to punish those who believe in him to suffer eternal damnation. On the contrary, he wants them near to him forever. Through faith we are saved.

Isn't that wonderful? That's also what he said to that sinful woman. He says to her that her faith has saved her. For she believed in the Lord Jesus. She is put in a restored relationship with God through her faith.

And it is only through faith that you can forgive others; faith in the Lord Jesus Christ, who lifts all burdens from our shoulders and who loves us unconditionally. Who strengthens us and gives us hearts full of compassion for others.

If you believe in the Lord Jesus, you can and will forgive others. If you believe in Jesus, you are a new person, full of joy and kind-heartedness.

Note well that in our passage in verse 37, Luke says that the woman *was* a sinner. Jesus uses the past tense. That is how she was, but that is not how she is any longer. She has repented from her sins.

That doesn't mean that she doesn't sin anymore. Of course not. But it does mean that she wants to live her life out of grace. It means that now she will do her utmost no longer to go back to her old lifestyle. She is a changed person. She has a different focus in her life. Her heart has changed. She has been reborn.

There is evidence of God's grace in her.

No doubt that evidence will also show in the way that she now treats her neighbour, not judgementally as the Pharisees do, but with compassion and love.

That is also what God wants from us: to forgive others and to have a heart of compassion, understanding, and love.

And if you know how sinful you yourself are, then that is not really all that hard. For then the Lord God has opened your eyes to the truth; to the truth of who you really are, how others truly are, and how they stand in relationship to the Lord our God.

Focus your life on the Lord Jesus and what he has done for you. And you will have peace, and you will be eternally joyful and thankful.

Reflection

1. Psalm 139:23–24 states, "Search me, O God, and know my heart! Try me and know my thoughts! And see if there be any grievous way in me, and lead me in the way everlasting!" Is your confidence in Christ great enough that you're not afraid to pray to God to open your eyes to the deeply flawed, often sinful ways you view others?

2. In what aspects of your life do you practically need the grace of God to help you forgive others, as well as to treat others with dignity and respect?

Chapter 9
Grief and Suffering Amid Adversity

"Truly, truly, I say to you, whoever hears my word
and believes him who sent me has eternal life.
He does not come into judgment,
but has passed from death to life."
John 5:24

"In the midst of life, we are in death."
Book of Common Prayer

"Man is like a breath;
his days are like a passing shadow."
Psalm 144:4

Introduction

Disease and death can suddenly make their unwelcome appearance, causing havoc and upheaval and disrupting the world as we know it. Everybody, in one way or the other, will encounter such disruption.

That is what my wife, children, and I experienced when our youngest son, a married father with three little boys, was afflicted with a rare autoimmune disease of the brain that rendered him a quadriplegic, unable to move or speak (see Introduction). Writing and delivering the sermon below, using as text Luke 8:54–

55, was a great help to me as we dealt with the many ramifications of our son's sudden affliction. It reminded me to be patient and to trust in God, for, as the apostle Peter writes, we should "not be surprised at the fiery trial when it comes upon you to test you, as though something strange were happening to you. But rejoice insofar as you share Christ's sufferings, that you may also rejoice and be glad when his glory is revealed" (1 Peter 4:12–13). Our grieving must be done in the sure knowledge that God has a purpose for everything and that he is the God of life, especially eternal life for all those who believe in him.

In our grieving, let's hold onto the unwavering understanding of God's nature—as the God of life with a perfect plan, even when it eludes our comprehension. God has pledged to transform all our sufferings. For all those who love him and believe in him he turns those sufferings, in one way or another, into something good. As Paul makes clear in Romans 8:28, "And we know that for those who love God all things work together for good, for those who are called according to his purpose."

In this chapter, we learn about the great healing power of the Lord Jesus, who is the only one who can truly comfort us.

Scripture

Luke 8:40–56

40 Now when Jesus returned, the crowd welcomed him, for they were all waiting for him.

41 And there came a man named Jairus, who was a ruler of the synagogue. And falling at Jesus' feet, he implored him to come to his house,

42 for he had an only daughter, about twelve years of age, and she was dying. As

Jesus went, the people pressed around him.

43 And there was a woman who had had a discharge of blood for twelve years, and though she had spent all her living on physicians, she could not be healed by anyone.

44 She came up behind him and touched the fringe of his garment, and immediately her discharge of blood ceased.

45 And Jesus said, "Who was it that touched me?" When all denied it, Peter said, "Master, the crowds surround you and are pressing in on you!"

46 But Jesus said, "Someone touched me, for I perceive that power has gone out from me."

47 And when the woman saw that she was not hidden, she came trembling, and falling down before him declared in the presence of all the people why she had touched him, and how she had been immediately healed.

48 And he said to her, "Daughter, your faith has made you well; go in peace."

49 While he was still speaking, someone from the ruler's house came and said, "Your daughter is dead; do not trouble the Teacher any more."

50 But Jesus on hearing this answered him, "Do not fear; only believe, and she will be well."

51 And when he came to the house, he allowed no one to enter with him, except Peter and John and James, and the father and mother of the child.

52 And all were weeping and mourning for her, but he said, "Do not weep, for she is not dead but sleeping."

53 And they laughed at him, knowing that she was dead.

54 But taking her by the hand he called, saying, "Child, arise."

55 And her spirit returned, and she got up at once. And he directed that something should be given her to eat.

56 And her parents were amazed, but he charged them to tell no one what had happened.

The Role of Faith?

Facing death is an agonizing experience, especially when it concerns a young person who is your own child, your own flesh and blood. Such a loss shakes you to the very core of your being, compelling you to go to any lengths to preserve that life.

That is certainly how it was with Jairus. This man is desperate. His twelve-year-old daughter is about to die. He will do anything to keep her alive. He will strip himself of his dignity if he must. He is at his wit's end.

That is how most people feel in a situation like that described by Luke. But that is especially the case for those who do not believe that there is life after death. To them, death is final.

For those of us who are Christians, that is different. We believe in the Lord Jesus and know that, even though we die, we will live. It appears that Jairus believes in the Lord Jesus. For that is to whom he goes for healing. But why does he believe in him? Does he believe that Jesus is the Son of God? Does he believe that he is the Saviour of the world and that he alone has power over all life and death? Or does he believe in him only because he performs miracles?

And so, we come to the key question, "What kind of faith must you have to save you? What exactly is the role of faith?" This passage teaches us that you cannot be healed without true faith. You must believe that Jesus is always true to his word, is the great Healer, and is the Almighty Son of God.

Jesus Is Always True to His Word

Wherever the Lord Jesus went, great crowds followed him. No wonder, for he performed so many miracles. He healed many. People came from all over to be cured.

But why did he do this? Why did Jesus go about healing? Was it just to cure physical ailments? No, it was more than that. It was an act of love and a reflection of a new and better world. It was a means to an end. He wanted to create true faith in the hearts of the people and to teach them about the resurrection and the way to eternal life. That takes time. It is not easy for us, flawed human beings, to gain insight. And so patience is needed. The Lord wants us to wait for him.

When Jairus comes to Jesus, he does so because he is in great distress. His daughter is at the point of death. In front of the whole crowd, this man drops to his knees and pleads with Jesus to come to his house and lay his hands on his daughter to heal her.

It is quite something that this man came to the Lord Jesus and did what he did, for we are told that he is a ruler of the synagogue. Such a person had quite a prominent position in Israel. He was part of the elite of society and highly regarded, for he presided over the board of the synagogue, which had jurisdiction over many matters. He also conducted and had control over the worship services. He counted the Scribes and the Pharisees among his friends. In terms of earthly power, he belonged to an influential group of people.

Jesus was not part of that group. They didn't like him. They considered him an outsider. An irritant. They didn't want him because he did not play according to their rules.

And now that prominent citizen falls to his knees before the Lord Jesus. It shows his desperation. But it also indicates that he believes in Jesus's healing power. He had heard all about it. All kinds of reports had gone out about his miraculous healing powers.

Therefore he asks Jesus to come and lay his hands on his daughter. It could be that he has a definite ritual in mind which would, as if by magic, make that happen. Jesus, without saying anything, goes with the ruler of the synagogue in the direction of his house.

However, the advance toward the ruler's house is painfully slow. A great crowd continues to press around Jesus to impede his progress. This, no doubt, is to the chagrin of the ruler of the synagogue. He is anxious about the fate of his daughter and wants Jesus to drop everything to help him. And so he urges him to get moving. In Luke 8:49, the term "troubling" is used, which means bothering, harassing or annoying someone. He is a man of authority who is used to having his requests honoured expeditiously and wants Jesus to get there before his daughter dies.

But that does not happen. Instead, an incident takes place which further delays Jesus. A woman who had been subject to bleeding for twelve years comes up behind him and touches the edge of Jesus's cloak in the hope of being healed. The text does not tell us precisely what the cause of her problem was. We know from Mark's account (5:26) that she had suffered much at the hands of physicians. She had spent everything she had for a cure.

Some commentators say that the suffering at the hands of the doctors was probably due to the kinds of remedies they prescribed in cases such as that. For example, one treatment would consist of a dose of Persian onions cooked in wine administered with the summons, "Arise out of your flow of blood." Another prescription would be to administer sudden shock or to carry the ash of an ostrich's egg in some cloth. But no one could heal her (Luke 8:43). Her case was hopeless.

This was especially difficult for her, not just because of the illness itself but also because her flow of blood made her perpetually unclean. According to the law of the Old Testament (Leviticus

15:19–22), the hemorrhage made her ceremonially defiled and unable to participate in the religious life of the nation. Someone who is unclean would be an outcast. All the beds, chairs, saddles, and vessels such a person touched were also declared unclean, as was any person who touched her. And so, marital intimacy would also be impossible. A woman with a continual flow of blood would remain barren.

As such, that is bad enough on its own. But added to that, she would not be allowed to go into the temple either, to church. That was forbidden for her.

Can you imagine if we were not allowed to do that? A few years ago, we were restricted because of the COVID-19 pandemic. We all looked forward to getting things back to normal and worshiping with a full church as before. But can you imagine if you could not go at all for the rest of your life? All your friends and family can go, but not you. You are considered unclean, an outcast.

This had been going on for twelve years. She was not allowed to participate in the communion of saints and experience the same privileges as others. She led a tortured and lonesome existence.

At this point, she was a desperate woman, hungry for a cure. She had been waiting for a long time. And so, what does she do? Well, she had also heard about Jesus. She knew that he heals the sick and was now in her neighbourhood. She had faith in him. She thought that if only she could touch him, then she would be healed, for she did not want to draw any attention to herself. And so she touches him. Secretly. She doesn't want anybody to notice, including Jesus.

But Jesus does notice. Therefore, he asks, "Who touched me?" This question seems pointless to the disciples, for the crowds were all around him and pressing him. Many people touched him.

The disciples were swept along by the emotionally charged atmosphere surrounding the impending death of the daughter of Jairus. They knew that a little girl was dying and that, of all people, only Jesus could do something about it. They are irritated because of the interruption. They want him to hurry up and get on with it. And now this.

But Jesus does not allow himself to be rushed.

Do you know why? Well, he did not want the woman to escape without her fully realizing why she was healed. Her faith made her well. Of course, it was not a perfect faith, far from it. And it was not so either that her faith as such saved her. It was the Lord Jesus who did that. But he would not have healed her if she had not believed.

Indeed, without faith, she would not even have sought Jesus out. What would have been the use if she did not believe he could do such a thing? She believed. That is why she acted.

But her faith had to be stronger than it was at that moment. Jesus does not rush because he wanted the woman to put her faith into action and not to keep her faith to herself. For that is what she wanted to do. She wanted to remain incognito. She did not want anybody to know about her situation.

And that is understandable. She was petrified. For what business did she have in touching the garment of the Lord Jesus? She was a persona non grata, an untouchable. And she was painfully aware of that.

However, after she touched Jesus's garment, things had changed. Jesus had made her well and taken away her reproach. It was no longer necessary to remain in hiding. Her faith had made her well. And that is what she had to acknowledge.

Faith is never just a private matter between you and God. No, our faith must be evident to our brothers and sisters and to those outside the family of God. Our faith means nothing if we cannot share it with others. True faith drives away fear. She had to realize and acknowledge that.

Jesus does not rush either because he wants Jarius to increase the strength of his faith. Just as he had in mind for the woman, Jesus was aiming at the heart of this prominent man. He wanted him to have just as strong a sense of faith as the woman. That cannot be done in a moment, in a flash. No, it is a process. Faith must be nurtured and strengthened. It must be steadfast. Not just for the moment. And it must have the right focus: Jesus Christ and the power of his resurrection.

For that reason, Jesus made this man think about the meaning of what had just happened with this woman and made him understand the significance of what was about to take place in his own house. For what was Jairus after? He just wanted Jesus to hurry up and make his daughter well again.

That is what we all want, don't we, when someone is sick and dying? Sickness interrupts our lives, what we're doing. It wreaks havoc with our agenda. It's an unwelcome visitor. The sooner it is gone, the better things are.

That's how it was with Jairus as well. He wanted to be able to get on with life. He had hopes and aspirations for his daughter. He did not want those to be taken away from him.

But then, as all of this is going on, someone from the house of Jairus comes and tells him that it is all too late. The girl had died. "Don't trouble the teacher any longer," they say. "Come on home with us so that you can mourn the death of your child. There is nothing that can be done. The girl is dead." Their thinking is dead is dead. Once a person dies, there is no longer any hope.

But carefully note the reaction of the Lord Jesus. Or his non-reaction. For what does he do? As is clear from the parallel passage in Mark 6:36, he pretends that he did not even hear what they said. It is as if they had not spoken a word. Jesus ignores them. Again, Jesus takes his time.

He demands patience for a very good reason. For by his actions he is teaching everyone, all of us, something especially important. Instead of addressing those who came from the house of Jairus, he speaks to Jairus directly. He says something incredibly significant. He says, "Do not fear; only believe, and she will be well."

Those are the same kinds of words spoken at important moments in the history of redemption. Those are the words the angel spoke to Mary when he announced the impending birth of the Lord Jesus. And that is also what the angel said to shepherds when Jesus's birth was announced. "Don't be afraid, just believe."

And now the Lord Jesus speaks these words because something very momentous is also about to occur. "Do not fear; only believe." Jesus was especially concerned about the faith of Jairus. He wants him to listen carefully to the words that he speaks. For as a man of his word, he speaks the words of truth. Every word he utters counts. He is the Word become flesh. He is the living Word. He is the one who fulfils the Scriptures. He is the one who makes all the promises contained in the Bible come true. And therefore, we have to listen to him. And trust in him, especially during times of extreme difficulty.

This is a pivotal teaching moment for Jairus. Jesus wants him to know that he is a man of his word. Always. Whatever he says will happen, *will* happen. He is totally and absolutely reliable. And what is more, his words are powerful. They have great significance. He never comes with empty platitudes, with some well-worn phrases appropriate just for the moment. No, the words he speaks are immensely powerful, effective and true.

Whatever he says will always happen. But he wants Jairus and all of us to know that he makes everything happen in *his* time.

Jairus thought that he could set the time schedule for when his daughter would be healed, and even how she would be healed. But Jesus teaches him to be patient. To wait for him. To watch him at work. Jairus had to listen carefully to the words that the Lord Jesus speaks.

The same thing is true for us.

Jesus's words are the words of life. Through his word, he creates faith in the heart of the hearer. And that is what the Lord Jesus is aiming for with Jairus. He is aiming for Jairus and all other believers to grasp the full significance of his divine power. He wants him to trust. He wants him to trust that he alone can bring about true healing.

But he is not only a prophet who speaks but also a man of action who does what he says. He is also the healer of Israel who restores life through his miraculous healing power.

Jesus as Healer

Finally, Jesus comes to the house of Jairus. Despite the sombre message about the child's death, he enters his home. He does not allow anyone to go with him, except for Peter, John, and James, and of course, the father and the mother. We are not told why. It could be that it was not practical. Although Jairus, as the ruler of the synagogue, would have been a wealthy man with good accommodations, the house nevertheless could have been too small for a large crowd.

It is significant that Jesus takes along those three apostles.

They are some of the more prominent disciples. The Scriptures say that the truth shall be established on the testimony of two or more witnesses. These disciples had to be witnesses so they could later tell others about it. So that they could write it down and pass on the words and actions of the great Healer, the Lord Jesus Christ, to the whole world. Because they were there at that time, we now have this account before us as well.

And what did they witness? It was about an hour after the girl breathed her last. As they followed Jesus into the house of Jairus, they encountered many relatives and mourners who were hired for the occasion. For that was the custom in those days. Mourners were hired to lament, weep, beat their breasts, and play mournful tunes. This was a duty of love to the one who had died.

It was thought that lamentation and burial had atoning power of its own. At that time, they even believed that the deceased person perceives everything until the stone is rolled before the tomb. And so such loud wailing and crying and going on were done especially for the benefit of the deceased person.

Jesus walked in while all that was going on. The burial rituals were already in full swing.

But now, what does Jesus do? He says something quite remarkable. He speaks precious words, beautiful words. Amid all the wailing and crying, he says, "Do not weep, for she is not dead but sleeping."

No one immediately grasps the meaning of these words, especially not those who were hired for the occasion. They think it's a cruel hoax. For what did they do? They suddenly turned from mourning to laughter, derisive laughter. They did not believe him. They were only doing what was expected of them. Her death had not really touched them. Their mourning was not genuine. It was only an empty ritual. To them, death is death. They were used to it.

That is the way it is with people in today's world as well. People are dying all the time; it doesn't stir them. Except, of course, when it is one of their own. Then they are inconsolable. Often, they are angry and full of dismay. They're looking to blame someone or something. When one of their loved ones dies, they are confronted with their own mortality. They're afraid of death. That is because they think that the life they live now is all they have. And that's why they hang on for dear life to the here and now.

But Jesus teaches these people and us about the reality of life and death. He teaches everyone to have a heavenly perspective. His actions demonstrate that God alone has power over life and death.

And so, he puts everyone outside except the father, mother, and the three disciples, and enters the young girl's room. He takes her by the hand and says, "Child, arise. Get up!" As soon as he had spoken these words, she rose and began to walk around.

What a beautiful and tender moment! What a tremendous happening! What a moment full of significance! She was dead, and now she is alive. They are dumbfounded. As Jesus wanted them to do, they asked themselves, "How can this be?" He wants them to observe.

As he addresses the little girl, he speaks tender words to her. Normally he would speak in Greek, but now Jesus uses the intimate and familiar language spoken in the home. Mark gives us the Aramaic words Jesus spoke: "*Talitha kumi.*" He used the words a loving father would use to wake his daughter up: "My dear girl, please wake up." These are tender words. These are words of love.

They show us that the Lord Jesus Christ, as shepherd and prophet, is true to his word, and that as healer, he restores the little girl's life. With this, he also shows that he is the Lord of creation and that, as Lord, he rules all things.

Jesus as Lord

What happened here in the home of Jairus was incredibly significant. The restoration of life is something quite remarkable, especially when that happens to a young girl whose whole life, humanly speaking, is still before her.

But that fact of restoration is still only a minor detail. For what does the raising of the daughter of Jairus point to? It points to the fact that Christ has power over life and death. It points to the fact that every life here on earth is in his hands. It points to *our* glorious resurrection. He is the one who creates life. He created your life, my life. He alone has the power over life and death.

We rely on doctors, nurses, and hospitals to prolong life. It is a great blessing that we have these people and these institutions of care, but their powers are so limited. There is so much they don't know. There is so much that they can't do. Ultimately, it is the Lord Jesus who controls our lives and our destiny. He knows how many days, hours, minutes, and seconds we have here on this earth. It's all in his loving hands.

Jesus wanted Jairus to trust him. To wait for him. He wanted him to know what a mighty God he is. He wanted him to know that there is more than life here on this earth. He wanted him to know that through faith you can have true life, eternal life.

He wanted to shake Jairus to the core of his being as he watched his daughter die.

And that's what Jesus wants to do with every one of us. All of us face death at one point or another. Whether of a loved one or our own. When that happens, God upsets our earthly lives. To make us think. To make us think about what life is truly all about. To make us realize that life is about our relationship with the Almighty God. And how wonderful and how vital that is. And how that relationship with God must be worked out in a relationship with each other, with our loved ones, with our brothers and sisters in the Lord, and with our fellow human beings.

God has created us to praise his name. And we have to do that here on this earth and into eternity. That is why he gave life to us. To praise him.

And so the critical concept with the raising of Jairus's daughter is not that Jesus restored her earthly life. For even after he raised her from the dead, she remains subject to death.

As we know from Romans 5, death came into the world because of sin. Adam and Eve were disobedient to the Lord God. And that is why they and their offspring, including us, deserve to die. The sentence of death now lies over all of creation—also today. But death was not part of the original plan of creation. Death is not natural; it is unnatural.

But now, by raising this little girl, the Lord Jesus Christ shows that he has power over death. He knows that he is about to pay the penalty of death and that he is about to be victorious over death. By raising this little girl from the dead, he is pointing to his coming resurrection. Jesus will die. But by his own power, he will also raise himself, and be raised, from the dead, so that those who belong to him will also know the resurrection and the life.

But, without faith, you cannot be saved. With the raising from the dead of this little girl, he wants to teach his disciples, Jairus, and his family that he is the One they have been waiting for, the Messiah; he who will save his people from their sins. He wants to teach them that he is the resurrection and the life.

The important thing is not that he has given this little girl back her earthly life. No, as I said, one day, she still will die again. She will not live forever on this earth. But through faith in the Lord Jesus Christ, she will have eternal life. That is the great hope she has and that we may have as well, if only we believe.

It will take some time before his disciples and all the others understand all this fully. It has to sink in.

That was the case not just for the disciples at that time but also for you and me. Time and again, God confronts us with the frailty of human life. He did that to the whole world a few years ago with COVID-19. Many people were very anxious and afraid. That's understandable. The possibility and the inevitability of death are frightening. For all of us. That is why we must always remember to put our faith in God. Oh, sure, we need to take precautions. We cannot live recklessly. But we do not need to be anxious. We need to trust in God and have faith in him, who is the author of life.

Jesus says to all those who are grieving the loss of a loved one or staring death in the face the same thing as he said to Jairus: "Don't be afraid, just believe. Wait for me. Trust me. I am the Almighty God who alone has power over life and death."

Reflection

1. Consider the various ways that faith is present in our lives over time and in different circumstances—from milestone events such as the joy of birth to the daily blessings of a long walk outdoors. Then consider how faith sustains us during times of grief. How does faith save us during these times of loss? Following 1 Peter 4:12–13, reflect on the ways that God's goodness is revealed in his presence across the spans of our lives.

2. What specific challenges do you face when called to place your trust in Jesus with your whole heart and mind? Reflect on these challenges and imagine how your life—and the lives of those around you—would change were you to overcome these challenges through faith in your Lord and Saviour Jesus Christ.

Chapter 10
God Is Our Refuge at All Times

*"He who dwells in the shelter of the Most High
will rest in the shadow of the Almighty.
I will say of the LORD,
'He is my refuge and my fortress,
my God, in whom I trust.'"*

Psalm 91:1–2

*"Who shall separate us from the love of Christ?
Shall tribulation, or distress, or persecution, or famine,
or nakedness, or danger, or sword?
As it is written, 'For your sake we are being killed all
the day long;
we are regarded as sheep to be slaughtered.'
No, in all these things we are more than conquerors
through him who loved us.
For I am sure that neither death nor life,
nor angels nor rulers, nor things present nor things to
come,
nor powers, nor height nor depth,
nor anything else in all creation,
will be able to separate us from the love of God
in Christ Jesus our Lord."*

Romans 8:35–39

Introduction

At the time of writing this, on February 6, 2023, images of great destruction and mayhem flashed on the news channels because of an earthquake in southern Turkey and northern Syria. It is estimated that more than 15,000 people have been killed and many more injured. The damage, pain, and suffering are enormous.

This incident shows that a disaster can happen at any time. This earth is subject to floods, volcanic eruptions, hurricanes, fires, tornadoes, war, and disease. Our earthly lives are always in danger. We can never be sure of what the future will bring. This can make us anxious and afraid.

That is why I wrote this chapter. When a calamity happens, God's people need to be reassured and know that no matter what happens, God is always with them. They must also know how to respond. They must believe in him, and worship him and put their lives into his hands. They must know as a certainty that as long as they believe, their relationship with God can never be broken.

This chapter is based on Psalm 46, which describes similar calamitous times. It is not known exactly what the occasion was for this Psalm, but many scholars believe that it was the frightening time described in 2 Chronicles 32, where we read about the miraculous deliverance of God's people in Jerusalem after Sennacherib (745 BC–681 BC), king of Assyria, invaded Judah in 700 BC, blasphemed the Lord God, and threatened to destroy Jerusalem.

Scripture

Psalm 46

To the choirmaster.

Of the Sons of Korah.

According to Alamoth.

A Song.

1 God is our refuge and strength, a very present help in trouble.

2 Therefore we will not fear though the earth gives way, though the mountains be moved into the heart of the sea,

3 though its waters roar and foam, though the mountains tremble at its swelling.
Selah

4 There is a river whose streams make glad the city of God, the holy habitation of the Most High.

5 God is in the midst of her; she shall not be moved; God will help her when morning dawns.

6 The nations rage, the kingdoms totter; he utters his voice, the earth melts.

7 The LORD of hosts is with us; the God of Jacob is our fortress.
Selah

8 Come, behold the works of the LORD, how he has brought desolations on the earth.

9 He makes wars cease to the end of the earth; he breaks the bow and shatters the spear;

he burns the chariots with fire.

10 "Be still, and know that I am God. I will be exalted among the nations, I will be exalted in the earth!"

11 The LORD of hosts is with us; the God of Jacob is our fortress.
Selah

Trouble Brewing

As I noted above, the background of this Psalm indicates that Judah and God's people were in serious trouble. They were about to be annihilated by the greatest army of the time. The Assyrians had already invaded Judah and brutally taken over the fortified city of Lachish. Now, their troops were all around Jerusalem. Sennacherib, the king of the Assyrians, had previously defeated many other nations. There was no stopping him. He appeared invincible.

Can you imagine how the people would have felt at that time? The situation looked hopeless. God's people were about to lose everything: their city, the temple, their homes, their children, and their very lives.

We also live in tumultuous times. Life for many of us is nothing compared to what the Jerusalemites were going through at that time. There are no hostile armies standing at our borders. Our lives are not being directly threatened. But for others, death is present in their lives each day. Currently, our Ukrainian brothers and sisters are under assault in ways that recall the hostility of the Assyrians. Across the world, there is unrest against God and his authority—and the authority he has established on this earth.

We are not safe.

This uncertainty, truth be told, is the way it has been throughout the ages. There is political upheaval and uncertainty. Now, we are still suffering from the aftermath of a global pandemic that began on March 11, 2020, when the World Health Organization declared COVID-19 highly infectious. Frequently, we hear about floods caused by tropical storms or hurricanes, tsunamis, and earthquakes. Sometimes, thousands upon thousands of people are killed in one brief moment. At times like that there is much suffering and death.

People react to such disasters in different ways. But how should we as Christians react? Or an even better question: how does the Lord teach us to react? This question of reaction—what is expected of us—is addressed in Psalm 46.

This Psalm is divided into three sections, as indicated by the three *selahs* after verse 3, verse 7, and verse 11. Scholars are not entirely sure what that little word *selah* means, but it is generally believed that the word signals a musical rest in which the singers stop and during which time only the instruments are heard. It likely indicates a musical crescendo followed by a silent reflection. When you have a *selah*, then you have a pause, an interlude, a moment for meditation. We will follow this threefold outline as found in Psalm 46, namely that God is our protector, our Immanuel, and our exalted God.

God as Our Protector

This Psalm was sung in the temple in Jerusalem. It is likely that the refrain "God is our refuge" or "fortress" was sung by women. As indicated in the heading of this Psalm, *Alamoth* refers to women. When they sang that refrain, attention was drawn to each verse. In this way that central thought of God as our refuge is woven through each verse.

This Psalm is ultimately about the safety that people experience within the city of God, Jerusalem. Difficult to conquer, Jerusalem was a safe city. It was built on a hill, and those within the city could see the enemy coming. Jerusalem also had strong walls to protect it.

But, unlike other cities in the ancient Near East, Jerusalem only had a well from which the people might draw water. And that well was outside of the city.

Water is important. We cannot live long without it. That is why first responders give water to survivors of earthquakes and other disasters as soon as they emerge from the ruins. When the water supply is cut off, we are in trouble.

And so, even though Jerusalem is a safe city, its residents were still vulnerable there. When the water supply is easily cut off, disaster can easily overtake us.

You are not safe.

Indeed, there is no city in the world that can consider itself safe from any harm. When an earthquake occurs, the walls of the buildings come tumbling down. When tornadoes or tsunamis come, property can be destroyed in seconds.

When riots break out, as frequently happens in various parts of the world, property can be looted and destroyed, and lives put at risk. So, no matter the source, time, or cause, there is no safety in any city or man-made structure.

You never know when God is going to take everything away, including your life.

Our earthly lives are hanging by a thread.

Does that mean then that we are not safe? Not at all. The Psalmist assures us that God is his refuge and strength. He doesn't depend on the walls of Jerusalem. He doesn't depend on the fortifications. He doesn't depend on the water supply. God alone is his refuge.

The word translated as *refuge* in verse 1 means a shelter in which people seek shelter in severe weather, or from dangers as they travel through the high hills. The word in verses 7 and 11 means "a stronghold, a high tower, a fortress." Both words refer to the same concept: God is a refuge on which all can depend, even when everything around us seems to be falling apart.

No doubt there are many fears in our lives. We wonder at times whether some disaster can also happen to us, or whether we will perish in some accident or find ourselves in the wrong place at the wrong time. Across the world, the very foundations of civil society seem to quake. There is so much division and turmoil and strife.

We fear many other aspects of our lives. We fear for our health, the health of our children, and the health of an unborn baby. We wonder whether we can go on and whether or not we are able to do all that is expected of us. And we worry.

Will we be safe?

To be safe, we can do as the Psalmist says: go to the Lord for shelter. He is a very present help in trouble. He is not sleeping, and he is alive right now. He watches over us like a mother over her child.

God is always in control. He is always on his throne with his Son beside him. He is the Almighty God who has a plan for his creation. And everything is worked out in that plan. Each and every one of us is part of God's plan. Our lives are in his loving hands.

The Psalmist says that he will not fear, even though the earth gives way and the mountains be moved into the heart of the sea. The author is imagining the worst calamity that could possibly hit his people as he describes earthquakes, volcanoes erupting, and mountains crashing into the sea.

He paints a picture here of chaos and tumult and terrifying noises. This is what we witness every time there is a strong earthquake or tornado or flood or tsunami. When we are in the midst of such a calamity, we think it is the end of the world.

But it isn't.

In essence, a calamity is God giving the world another chance to turn to him. That is what any calamity or pandemic calls for.

That is what the Lord Jesus said in Luke 13:2-5 in recalling the Galileans who were killed by the Romans. He said, "Do you think that these Galileans were worse sinners than all the other Galileans, because they suffered in this way? No, I tell you; but unless you repent, you will all likewise perish."

Luke goes on to speak about eighteen Jews on whom the tower in Siloam fell and killed them. He says, "Do you think that they were worse offenders than all the others who lived in Jerusalem? No, I tell you; but unless you repent, you will all likewise perish."

Calamities warn us and bring us to repentance. Our Lord wants us to bear fruit, especially the fruit of repentance. And, yes, the final destruction of this world is going to come. The entire world is going to be burned up and destroyed. That will indeed happen on the last day (2 Peter 3:7).

But until that day comes, the Lord keeps beckoning us to call upon him and to seek shelter with him. He tells us that it is important for us to turn to him and to place our trust in him rather than the present circumstances of the world. As we read in Psalm 27:1-2, "The LORD is my light and my salvation; whom shall I fear? The LORD is the stronghold of my life; of whom shall I be afraid? When evildoers assail me to eat up my flesh, my adversaries and foes, it is they who stumble and fall."

Do you believe these words when you read them or sing them? Do you mean them? Does that meaningfulness show for all to see?

Jesus Is Our Saviour

A greater miracle than the defeat of the Assyrian army happened just outside of Jerusalem some seven hundred years later, when Jesus Christ won the victory over death on Golgotha. No greater miracle has ever happened. That is a great comfort for us. In the midst of trouble, you can turn to him. He will save you.

Listen to what the Lord Jesus says in John 7:37–39: "If anyone thirsts, let him come to me and drink. Whoever believes in me, as the Scripture has said, 'Out of his heart will flow rivers of living water.'"

Only because of his shed blood is there any hope for this world. For after his death, he rose from the grave. And now anyone who believes in him also has the victory over death. There is more to this life here on earth.

We learn in verse 7 of this Psalm that the LORD of hosts is with us. In Hebrew, the text reads "*Yahweh Sabaoth Immanu.*" We hear the word *Sabaoth*. That phrase is also found in the Hymn of Luther: "A Mighty Fortress Is Our God." Luther used this Psalm as a template for his Hymn. He wrote, "Dost ask who that may be? Christ Jesus, it is He; Lord *Sabaoth* his name, from age to age the same, and He must win the battle."

Luther found himself frequently in very precarious circumstances. But he sought his refuge with God, with the Lord Sabaoth, the LORD of hosts. On the basis of this Psalm and all of God's Word, Luther realized that God is with us even though the nations are in an uproar—and even though kingdoms may fall.

The verb "rage" in verse 6 is the same word used in verse 3 to describe the roar of the waters. We have seen how destructive waters can be. We saw that in the 2011 tsunami of Japan, Great Tōhoku Earthquake. We saw a similar devastation with the effects of the 2004 tsunami in the Indian Ocean, with the destruction of approximately 90,000 buildings in Sri Lanka alone and the deaths of over 227,000 souls.

It says in the Psalm that when the Lord God utters his voice, the earth melts. In such disasters and pandemics, we must hear the voice of God. We must hear his call to repentance. We must hear the call to depend on him, the call to flee to him for deliverance, for security, and for safety. We often don't know why we must suffer or understand its purpose. That is the way it was for Job as well. But he hung on to God and persevered. And God brought him through his suffering. For there is only one way that you can be safe here on this earth, and that is if you find refuge with the Lord God, the Creator of heaven and earth.

As we are told in Psalm 125:1, "Those who trust in the LORD are like Mount Zion, which cannot be shaken but endures forever." Mount Zion refers to Jerusalem. It is the city of God where there is a river whose streams make glad the city of God. The Psalmist says that God is within her. In the Hebrew language, God is our Immanuel, which means our "God with us."

God Is Our Immanuel

We come here to our first *selah*, and therefore the Psalmist asks us to pause, to let that sink in: God is always with us. We will not fear though the earth gives way.

God's presence with us both endures and prevails.

Is it not curious that the Psalmist speaks here about a river whose streams make glad the city of God? As we saw, there is no river that runs through Jerusalem. There are no streams of water in Jerusalem.

The Psalmist is now speaking symbolically. With water, we sustain life. Water is the source of life. That is precisely what God is to his people. God is like a river running through Jerusalem. That is why the Psalmist speaks about a river whose streams make glad the city of God. By speaking here about a river that flows right through Jerusalem, the Psalmist wants us to realize that the Lord gives his people the assurance that he is the one who gives life to his people.

He protects their lives no matter what dire circumstances they find themselves in; no matter what may happen to them; no matter what dangers surround them; no matter how many enemies they face; no matter how precarious their health may be; no matter when they think they're about to die. With God, they are given life, eternal life. He is the God of the living. If we find our refuge with him, then everything is well with our children and with us.

As Sennacherib and his huge army surrounded Jerusalem, the people were assured that God would protect them. They need only trust him.

That sense of trust is what we read about in verse 5. God will help when morning dawns. That's exactly what happened. God came to help in a miraculous way. For the angel of the Lord in the night went through the camp of the Assyrian soldiers and killed 185,000 of them. We know from 2 Kings 19:36 that God, by his avenging angels, destroyed the army of Sennacherib. This mighty Assyrian king had to return to Nineveh, the capital of Assyria, beaten. Not long after, his two sons cut him down with the sword as he was worshiping in the temple of his god Nisroch. Sennacherib lost everything.

The Lord God rescued his people. God was their river and provided them with the water of life.

To be sure, water can either save us, or it can destroy us. It is all God's doing. Think about the water of the Red Sea (Exodus 14). It caused the death of many Egyptians, but it gave life to the people Israel. Water can bring safety, or it can bring destruction.

Upon further reflection, we recall that Isaiah also conjures up the image of a river. He says in Isaiah 33:20–21,

Behold Zion, the city of our appointed feasts! Your eyes will see Jerusalem, an untroubled habitation, an immovable tent, whose stakes will never be plucked up, nor will any of its cords be broken. But there the LORD in majesty will be for us a place of broad rivers and streams, where no galley with oars can go, nor majestic ship can pass.

Again, here, the Lord God is pictured as a river. And that river will supply the people with everything they need. Isaiah also speaks about ships on that river—in this case, warships, not pleasure crafts. He assures the people that those who seek to harm them will not be able to enter the city of God. God protects his own people.

What a great comfort this promise is to those who are perishing, to those who are about to perish. How God's people in Jerusalem must have rejoiced when they saw how they had been saved from disaster.

Some will say we do not see these kinds of miraculous interventions today. Where was God, for example, during the horrors of World War I and World War II? Where was he when millions of Jews were being incinerated in the gas chambers? Where was he in all these cruelties?

These are good questions to ask, for they make us think about the reason for pain and suffering. The Bible teaches us that these are the consequences of a world that has come under the devastating consequences of sin as we see in Genesis 3.

In the horrors of war, disasters, calamities, and pandemics, we must listen to what God tells us and hear the call to depend on him, to flee to him for deliverance, for security, and for safety.

We must hear his call to repentance.

For there is only one way that we can be safe here on this

earth, and that is if we find refuge with the Lord God, the Creator of heaven and earth.

To be safe, we must listen.

He Is Our Exalted God

Once again, we read in verse 7 that the LORD of hosts is with us; the God of Jacob is our fortress. Once again, the Psalmist has us pause. He says *Selah*. It is time to thank God again for his presence, to thank him that he is our fortress, in our exalted God.

In verse 8 we are summoned to see the works of the Lord and the desolations that he has brought on the earth. In the streets of American cities, during the protests and riots that occurred in the aftermath of George Floyd's death in 2020, we sometimes saw protesters and police together in impromptu prayer, calling upon God. It was a time for reflection, for understanding and connection with each other, but also for personal repentance.

For this is the kind of response God expects from us. He tells us to love him and to love our neighbour, to worship him and to repent.

Yet he also told us that nations will come in uproar and that they will be full of rage. Those who do not repent and want to follow their own way will vent their anger on those who stand in their way. That is the way it has been throughout the ages and will continue to be so. The Lord Jesus told of that sense of rage and chaos in Luke 21:10–11: "Nation will rise against nation, and kingdom against kingdom. There will be great earthquakes, and in various places famines and pestilences. And there will be terrors and great signs from heaven."

We should not be surprised at any of this. God has warned us, for look at what he has done and continues to do. In all these things we must recognize God's hand. He wants to turn whatever calamity comes upon us to our good. He promises to turn us from darkness to light.

It is important to understand that God does not want this misery and pain and sorrow to happen. God does not delight in human suffering. No, he is not the author of sin or the effects of sin.

The Lord God wants us to worship him and seek our salvation and well-being from his hands alone. Only he can bring restoration. Only he can bring true peace here on this earth.

He brought peace on the earth through his Son Jesus Christ, for the Lord Jesus Christ dealt with sin. He died for the sin of this world so that this world could be restored.

He beckons us to come to God and see what he can do. For when the Lord Jesus rose into heaven, he did not leave us alone. He gave us his Holy Spirit. He gave us the assurance of renewal.

Listen to what the Psalmist says in verse 9 and see what purpose God has with his all. He tells us that he makes wars cease to the ends of the earth, and that he breaks the bow and shatters the spear, and that he burns chariots with fire. He brings peace on earth by destroying the weapons of war. He is on his throne.

Our God Is the God of Peace and Justice

Whenever there are calamities all over the world, we have an opportunity to come with the Gospel. It is an opportunity to teach those affected by these painful happenings that God is warning them and all of us to lead a life of repentance—and that he is the One who alone can rescue this world from sin and misery.

But the prophecy of this Psalm also looks forward to the peace that will be established here on earth in the life hereafter. The time will come when there will be no more earthquakes, when there will then be no more wars, when there will be no more volcanic eruptions.

That is why we are looking forward to the new earth. We are looking forward to the time when our bodies will have been totally renewed and made indestructible. We are looking forward to the time when, as we learn in Revelation 22, Christ is the source of life to the fullest.

In Revelation 22 we read about the angel who showed John "the river of the water of life, bright as crystal, flowing from the throne of God and of the Lamb through the middle of the street of the city; also, on either side of the river, the tree of life with its twelve kinds of fruit, yielding its fruit each month. The leaves of the tree were for the healing of the nations."

Our Lord and Saviour Jesus Christ is the inexhaustible well from which we can drink forever and ever. We will never go hungry, and we will never go thirsty.

Returning to verse 10, we see how it calls us to bow before God who is exalted among the nations and in all the earth. The fact that he is exalted means that even though he is very much involved in this creation, he is nevertheless beyond it. He alone is worthy of adoration.

Again, God tells us to be still and know that he is God. He wants us to cease for a moment and to let our hands hang meaningfully by our sides as we leave things in God's hands. We must know God and the power of his Word and Spirit. We must trust that he is in control of all things.

We must be still.

That does not mean that we should not be doing anything. Not at all. But it does mean that we should let our hands hang by our sides as a symbol that we do not take up the weapons of war that the world uses. We do not engage in violence of any kind.

Instead, in the words of Ephesians 6:10-16, we put on the full armour of God and stand firm with a belt of truth buckled around our waist and with the breastplate of righteousness in place and our feet fitted with the readiness that comes from the gospel of peace. We take up the shield of faith with which we can extinguish all the flaming arrows of the devil. We must put on the helmet of salvation and the sword of the Spirit, which is the word of God. We pray for God to hear us and to rescue us.

He will hear us. We may hear people blaspheme his name now and trample on his covenant promises and demands. But this Psalm tells us that God will be exalted on the earth.

No matter when.

No matter what.

In the end, the Lord of hosts is with us, exalted among the nations—exactly as Psalm 46 reminds us. And what of those who do not believe? Here we may turn to John (3:16-21): "Whoever does not believe is condemned already, because he has not believed in the name of the only Son of God" (19). Those who hate the light "will be thrown into the outer darkness. In that place there will be weeping and gnashing of teeth" (12).

But for those who believe in him, it will be a tremendous day of triumph. For those who have trusted in him during this life, it will be a great day of joy. Even in the most calamitous times, God is always with us.

God will be exalted on the earth. He is our strength. He is our refuge. And we can safely flee to him.

Reflection

1. Be honest: what is the biggest fear in your life? How is that fear inconsistent with what you say you believe? How does Psalm 46 instruct you to be at peace?

2. Do you pray regularly to God to strengthen you in your faith, especially during difficult circumstances? Is your life more characterized by peace and contentment or fear?

Chapter 11
Comforting Those Who Are Dying or Grieving

*"The LORD is near to the brokenhearted
and saves the crushed in spirit."*
Psalm 34:18

*"Blessed are those who mourn,
for they shall be comforted."*
Matthew 5:4

Introduction

The topic of death and dying is not an easy one. We have many mixed emotions. We all know that we are going to die, but it's usually not a topic any of us is very comfortable with.

That's understandable. For who wants to focus on an enemy and on the hurt that the enemy will inflict on you? For that is what the Bible calls death: our enemy. We are told in 1 Corinthians 15: 25–26 that death is the last enemy to be conquered.

The Lord Jesus conquered that enemy, as that passage also states. He conquered death and everything to do with death and dying. But that is something we must believe. It is a faith that we must put into practice. And that's where the difficulty comes in.

Early in my ministry, I had to comfort a brother whose father died of a heart attack. This young brother was in his mid-thirties, and his father was in his seventies. And so it wasn't anything abnormal. And yet he was inconsolable. He became severely depressed and was not able to return to work for quite some time.

What was the problem? In talking to him, I learned that as a young boy he had lost his younger brother in an accident. He and his brother were playing on the driveway of his home, and his brother darted out onto the highway, chasing after a ball. He was hit by a car and killed instantly. It happened right in front of his eyes.

His parents, of course, were devastated. They made all the funeral arrangements and allowed themselves to be comforted by friends, relatives, and people from the church. But nobody paid any attention to the little boy whose little brother just died in front of him. Not even his parents.

When the time for the funeral came, he was not even invited to go and was left with a babysitter.

Why? Well, because the parents wanted to spare him the grief. They thought that it would be too painful for him to be there. They wanted him to forget about it as soon as possible. They did not believe that children understood all the consequences of death and that therefore, they would quickly get over it.

However, he never did get over it. It bothered him throughout his entire life, for he had not been allowed to grieve and to mourn. He had a lot of questions and had all kinds of guilt feelings which he tried to suppress. But he couldn't. He couldn't make sense of it all. Sadly, all these things came to the fore when his father died.

Here is what God teaches us in 1 Thessalonians 4:13: "Brothers, we do not want you to be ignorant about those who fall asleep, or to grieve like the rest of men, who have no hope." Somebody who does not know the Scriptures and the core message of the Bible will deal with grief in a worldly, physical way. That is what children will do because they do not have a complete understanding of the true nature of death and life. And so we need to teach them in the light of God's Word. But we also need to be taught because we easily grieve inappropriately and take over worldly myths.

Scripture

2 Corinthians 1:3–7

3 Blessed be the God and Father of our Lord Jesus Christ, the Father of mercies and God of all comfort,

4 who comforts us in all our affliction, so that we may be able to comfort those who are in any affliction, with the comfort with which we ourselves are comforted by God.

5 For as we share abundantly in Christ's sufferings, so through Christ we share abundantly in comfort too.

6 If we are afflicted, it is for your comfort and salvation; and if we are comforted, it is for your comfort, which you experience when you patiently endure the same sufferings that we suffer.

7 Our hope for you is unshaken, for we know that as you share in our sufferings, you will also share in our comfort.

Heidelberg Catechism

42. Q. Since Christ has died for us,
why do we still have to die?

A. Our death is not a payment for our sins,
but it puts an end to sin
and is an entrance into eternal life.[1]

[1] Jn 5:24; Phil 1:21–23; 1 Thess 5:9, 10.

43. Q. What further benefit do we receive
from Christ's sacrifice and death on the cross?

A. Through Christ's death
our old nature is crucified,
put to death,
and buried with him,[1]
so that the evil desires of the flesh
may no longer reign in us,[2]
but that we may offer ourselves to him
as a sacrifice of thankfulness.[3]

[1] Rom 6:5–11; Col 2:11, 12.
[2] Rom 6:12–14.
[3] Rom 12:1; Eph 5:1, 2.

Myths about Grieving

Myth 1: Grief and mourning are the same.

What is grief, and how is it different from mourning? Some people use these words interchangeably. But they're not the same. Grief is our human response to loss. Grief has to do with our inward thoughts and feelings as we process the loss of someone or something very dear to us. Grieving is usually a lifetime experience. There are so many things that remind us of our departed loved ones, and we wish they were still alive so that we could talk to

185

them again and tell them things that we wish we had said when they were still alive.

Mourning is the external expression of your grief. In the Old Testament, that included the tearing of clothes, the wearing of sackcloth, disfiguring oneself with dust and ashes, fasting, and the like. In those times, even professional mourners were employed. That was also the case in the New Testament (cf. Matthew 9:23, Mark 5:38). Today, we mourn not only at the graveside but also by keeping memorabilia, such as pictures and other physical reminders.

Myth 2: Children (and adults) only grieve for a short time and get over it in time.

What is grief? Grief is the pain you experience because of losing a loved one. As such, there are many emotions involved in this.

The sense of loss exists because your loved one is gone. You miss their companionship and the special relationship you had with them. Special events remind you of them, such as birthdays, anniversaries, Christmas, and holidays. Such events remind you of the times the loved one was still around. As time goes on, such pain diminishes. But the pain never totally goes away.

It is God's way of reminding us that what we have here on earth is temporary and that, ultimately, our citizenship is in heaven (Philippians 3:20). There, we will have full communion with him and all his saints. And it will be a perfect union. There will be no more pain or sorrow. There will never be the pain of separation from a loved one, either.

There are many other aspects to the grieving process. Sometimes, there are unresolved issues. For example, guilt because you did not treat your loved one as you think you should have.

186

Or guilt because you feel that, in one way or the other, you could have prevented their death.

Each person is unique and grieves in different ways because those who grieve have to deal with various issues unique to that individual. All these things need to be worked through. And you need someone to help you through that.

For children, the grieving process is more complicated. As children grow up, their understanding becomes greater. That is why it is so necessary to talk openly about things. And to be open to answering questions as they come up.

Myth 3: It is sinful to grieve and to mourn.

That's what some people think. But that's not true. Grieving and mourning are part of being image bearers of our Father in heaven. Think about it. The Lord God himself grieved and mourned. For example, in Genesis 6:5–6 we read, "The LORD saw that the wickedness of man was great in the earth, and that every intention of the thoughts of his heart was only evil continually. And the LORD regretted that he had made man on the earth, and it grieved him to his heart." With him it is a holy grief and sorrow over the broken relationship with his people. That fills his heart with pain. God grieves over the loss of communication with humankind.

The Lord Jesus himself also experienced grief in his lifetime. When he heard about the death of John the Baptist, he withdrew to grieve in a solitary place. He also wept at the grave of his friend Lazarus (John 11:33–36).

We on earth suffer loss all the time. We suffer the loss of possessions, health, life, and whatever belongs to this current earth. Why does that happen? It is good to grieve because God wants to remind us that our current possessions, including our earthly lives, are temporary. They are not meant to last. Sickness and death are a reminder that this earth is not our permanent and final abode. God has prepared a place in heaven for all who belong to him.

Myth 4: Burials are for close relatives only.

There is a trend nowadays to keep a burial service at the grave site, and even a funeral service, private. Only close relatives are allowed to come to the grave site. The reason they give is that they want to be able to express their grief privately. Only after the interment are distant relatives and friends and other people from the community allowed to come to a memorial service.

This is not necessarily wrong. Funerals are private affairs, and it is ultimately the family's decision and none of anyone's business. But it is good to reflect on this. What exactly is the reason?

If it is done because you don't want to mourn publicly, then I wonder, why not? Why are some people afraid to show their emotions in public? Do they think it is a sin or a sign of weakness, or a lack of faith? The Lord Jesus didn't think so. Nor should we.

And why not allow others to share this experience with you? Furthermore, close friends and others also want to be able to mourn.

Why should the actual burial be a private affair? Others also want to be there when their dear friend is lowered into the ground. It is an essential part of us coming to grips with the reality of death, with the fact that the person is no longer around. It reminds us of the great hope we have in the resurrection of the body and rising again from that grave. The symbolism of burial is enormously significant.

I like how funerals are held in Ontario, where I used to live. It is quite different from how it is done in the western provinces of Canada. In Ontario, friends and relatives are given an opportunity to extend their condolences at the funeral home or the church building a day or two before the actual funeral. People are invited to come to view the body in the casket, to share their grief and extend condolences. This is usually done in the evening so that people who would not be able to attend the funeral service, which is generally in the daytime, can still pay respect to the family of the departed one. In this way, so many more people can be a comfort to those who are grieving.

At the time of the death of my parents in Ontario, it was wonderful to see so many people before the funeral. They died about a year apart, first my father and then the following year my mother, and both times, there were so many people that the lineups took about two or three hours to pass by.

I'm incredibly grateful to my church council and my whole church community that they allowed me to take my time at the time of their deaths. There was no pressure on me to be back as quickly as possible. On the contrary, church members even sent flowers at the time of my mother's funeral. We all need time to mourn and to grieve and to have time to interact with our relatives and friends.

In the western provinces of Canada, except for a few family members and perhaps close friends, it is rare to have anybody come to the funeral home before the actual funeral. During my ministry in British Columbia and Alberta, I must've conducted at least forty or fifty funeral services. Since I was familiar with the way it was done in Ontario, I suggested that the grieving families also invite the church community to come to the funeral home. This meant more work for me as the minister, but seeing that this tradition is still being kept in those churches I served, I think it is much appreciated.

Children also need to be included. Why would you exclude them? A funeral gives a child the opportunity to be part of the mourning process. It allows adults and children to comfort each other and to honour the life of the person who has died. And so, they should be encouraged to attend. That does not mean that they should be forced. Ultimately, it should be their decision.

We all need to be reminded that we are dust and that to dust, we shall return (e.g., Ecclesiastes 3:20). We also need to have the visible reminder that the body is planted like a seed and that a most glorious body will rise from it again.

At a funeral I will often tell the people not just to look down into the grave but to look up, because Christ is going to come again. At that time, all the dead will rise from their graves. What a glorious day that will be!

That is the great hope we have at a time like that, which is also the great hope expressed especially at the burial site.

It is true, of course, that the closer you are to the person, the more it is necessary to go through all the forms of mourning. When you lose your wife or your husband of fifty years whom you loved dearly, or your parents, or a child, then the grief and the mourning will be so much greater.

It is normal to grieve. And to mourn. When you are in pain, such pain needs to be expressed. That is why the Lord God created us as a community together. We cannot exist in isolation. To exist in isolation from God and from others is what hell is all about.

Some time ago, I attended some lectures on counselling from Dr. Dan Allender. (He is a professor who has written much and whose focus is on sexual abuse and trauma, as well as recovery through story.) He spoke to us about the difficult childhood that he had had, and how that affected him and shaped him. His father was a cold and distant man. He was also an alcoholic. He did not have any friends and was not close to his wife and his children.

Allender found out why his father was that way just before his father died, when he spent a week with his dad while he was on his deathbed. And then, his father told him about his experiences as a soldier during World War II. He told him that a very dear and close childhood friend of his had been killed right beside him. This affected him profoundly. He was so full of pain and grief because of his friend's death that he decided never to again be close to anyone, for it was an experience that he never wanted to have again. He tried to forget about this experience and never talked about it. Consequently, he became a lonely and bitter man.

The problem is that we may try to forget the events, but we can never forget the feelings associated with the events. When a traumatized soldier, for example, who has never adequately dealt with the horror he has experienced, is in one way or the other reminded of those events, he will act unpredictably. For example, he may hear a car backfire and be right back in the war.

We need to deal with our pain and sorrow. When we suffer significant loss, we need to grieve and mourn. Otherwise, we will react in strange, painful, and destructive ways.

In 1969, the publication of Elizabeth Kubler-Ross's landmark text *On Death and Dying* hit the bookshelves. She popularized the concept of the five stages of dying and grieving: Denial, Anger, Bargaining, Depression, and finally, Acceptance.

However, she never intended that people should interpret her "five stages of dying" literally. Yet, that is what many have done. It is not so that the one stage naturally follows the other. No, you can go back and forth in those stages. And that is because we all process loss differently. And no two people are alike.

Myth 5: Children are too young to understand death and religious beliefs about death.

It is true that, depending on the age of a child, children do not have a complete understanding of death, of heaven, and of eternal life. That was brought home to me once when my dad visited me. We are of Dutch descent, and so my children called him *Opa* (which means "grandpa").

At that time, my youngest daughter had a friend over at our home whose own *Opa* had died quite some time ago. She did not remember him. She had heard her mom and dad talk about *Opa* a lot, but she didn't know what he looked like and had no personal recollection of him. All she knew was that her *Opa* had gone to heaven.

When she heard my daughter address my dad as *Opa*, her face lit up and she walked up to my dad and said, "Are you Opa? When did you get back from heaven?"

Children understand things literally. In a speech, Dr. Alan Wolfelt, who is one of North America's leading grief counsellors, gives the example of an eight-year-old girl who had been told that her grandfather had gone to heaven. She asked, "If Grandpa is in heaven, why did we put him in the ground?" It's good that that little girl dared to ask the question. That she did not think that she would be ridiculed or dismissed.

We should not assume that children know what we know. We should not assume that when we speak about heaven, they right away understand what we are talking about. We need to teach them as they grow up. And the older they become, the more they will understand.

That is why God gave them parents in the first place: to teach them theological concepts about very important things such as death and dying and the concept of body and soul. And the great hope that we have as Christians.

Pastoring the dying and the mourning is an important part of the minister's work, the elder and the deacon. It is challenging but also very rewarding. It is challenging because we often are at a loss as to how to attend to those who are dying and their loved ones. We need to know how to respond compassionately, scripturally, and truthfully. It is also rewarding because, during times like that, people are brought close, close to God and to one another.

Visiting the Sick and Dying

Words are important.
Often, people find it challenging to find the right words to say to someone who has recently experienced the loss of a loved one. They fear uttering words that might exacerbate the person's grief and deepen their sorrow.

Rather than stressing over your choice of words, focus on actively listening to what they share with you. Understand their needs and emotions and respond accordingly. If you're preoccupied with concerns about the visit and how to navigate it, the chances of saying something inappropriate increase.

When visiting those who are seriously ill and nearing the end of their lives, it's essential to concentrate on their needs and not your own. At times like this, they are not likely to be interested in hearing our personal stories. One of the most important things to do is to listen and be very observant. Ask about the person's welfare. Ask, "Are you in a lot of pain?" Try to get a genuine understanding of what they want to share with you. And so, repeat in different words what they say to you.

If they say, for example, "I'm really having a hard time with all this." You could say, "You find it difficult?" And if they answer in the affirmative, you can ask, "What exactly do you find so difficult?" Latch onto what they're saying and follow up. Get them to explain. Listen to keywords and then try to make sure you understand what those words mean to them. Don't make assumptions. Make sure you're on the same page.

Often, people make the mistake of thinking about what they will say next. They are so busy with that that they hardly hear what the other person is saying. In this way, you get a disconnect and are not having a meaningful conversation.

Pay attention not only to the words spoken but also to the person's body language and overall demeanour. If they appear uneasy or have trouble focusing due to pain or medication, keep things short and simple.

People are moved by genuine empathy, warmth, and sincerity rather than the specific words used. They find comfort in knowing that you genuinely care. Therefore, it's crucial to be authentic and sincere in your interactions.

Also, ask what their immediate needs are at this moment. It may be something very simple. Perhaps they like to have their bed turned up or down or to have their pillow adjusted. Try to make them as comfortable as possible so that you can have a bit of a conversation.

And don't invade their privacy by sitting on the bed. If there is no chair, ask where you can find one or else remain standing.

Ask them about the kinds of things that they are most worried about at that moment. Perhaps they are concerned about their wife or husband or children or their finances. Or maybe they want to talk about things that have happened in the past. Reminiscence can be very important during these times.

But they will only tell you these things if they're comfortable with you. If they don't know you very well, they will not confide in you. They will not confide in you either if you come across as judgmental, as distant, or as having everything together.

Don't talk too much. Those who are lonely and bored will appreciate any kind of companionship, including someone who can regale them with all sorts of stories and anecdotes. But most often, that is not the case. Your experiences and perspective on things do not necessarily match someone else's.

Life is a journey through the wilderness.

Frequently, the Bible describes our lives as a journey through the wilderness. Many Scripture passages speak about the path that we must walk on, the mountains that we must climb, and the valleys that we must go through. Israel's journey through the wilderness is especially an important biblical theme. And that journey has a lot to tell us about what our life here on earth is about.

God designed the Exodus journey to deliver his people from Egypt. God made his people go through all kinds of hardships and uncertainties to test them. To show them who they are and who God is. God wanted to teach them that they are totally dependent on him. And that is such a hard lesson for all of us to learn.

Sometimes, the term *liminal space* is used to describe our journey in life. It refers to the space or time you shift from one phase to another. Israel had to go from Egypt to the promised land. We have to go from the world of sin into the world of no

195

sin. Someone who is on their deathbed is often keenly aware of that journey.

Supporting the terminally ill and those nearing the end of their lives is crucial as they navigate their final journey. How can you achieve this? Certainly not by standing on the sidelines observing their struggles, nor by lecturing them on how to live through those challenges. Instead, be a fellow traveller in their wilderness. Essentially, strive to empathize with their pain, attempting to comprehend their experiences and share in their suffering.

It's a journey every one of us must undertake. Even as we sit by the bedside in apparent physical health, we are not exempt from the frailty of the human condition. Our bodies, too, are subject to decay, and we are all moving towards the same destination. We are all travellers on the path to our ultimate goal, and it's a shared journey and struggle for each of us.

Such a journey is often quite unsettling, especially as you struggle with your past. You go from the familiar to the unfamiliar. A believer knows and believes that they will be with the Lord in heaven. But first, you have to pass through that dark tunnel. And that can cause panic. You worry about what you leave behind and wonder what is ahead of you. But if God is integrated into the liminal moments in our lives, then we are better prepared for death.

Be willing to enter into the experience of the dying person. Don't be afraid of silences. And don't be scared either to address difficult emotions and existential questions they are struggling with.

Perhaps there are unconfessed sins from the past. Don't brush over them and dismiss them. When they bring up some serious indiscretion from the past, it is very important to let them speak about that. They need to be heard. Otherwise, they wouldn't bring it up. It's something they need to get off their chest, and if you quickly dismiss it, you don't do them as service at all. On the contrary.

Bring them the manna from heaven. In other words, comfort them with God's Word. The Psalms are wonderful for that. Speak to them about the forgiveness of sins for those who want to repent from their sins.

Right now, together, we are all on the road to our final destination, and we need to help each other and remind one another that this earth is not our final destination. God is preparing us for a new heaven and a new earth where he will dwell with us. He will wipe away every tear from our eyes, and "death shall be no more, neither shall there be mourning, nor crying, nor pain anymore, for the former things have passed away" (Revelation 21:3–4).

Reflection

1. Reflect on the transitional periods in your life and consider how you think about and approach daily living and how that aligns with the way that you prepare yourself and your loved ones for death. In each of these transitional moments, for instance, do you acknowledge the presence of God's hope as recounted in 1 Thessalonians 4:13?

2. What are the ways in which you can improve your interaction with others who are hurting? In the section above on the importance of words, you will find suggestions on language to use at times of loss. Reflect on times of loss in your life and consider how different

PROMISES UNBROKEN

types of language and actions might have been of
greater comfort to those with whom you were visiting.

Chapter 12
On Prayer

"Draw near to God, and he will draw near to you."
James 4:8

"Is anyone among you suffering . . . ?
Let him pray."
James 5:13

"Do not be anxious about anything,
but in everything by prayer and supplication
with thanksgiving
let your requests be made known to God."
Philippians 4:6

Introduction

In the Heidelberg Catechism, prayer is dealt with in the last section. Why? According to the catechism, prayer is the most important part of our thankfulness to God. If that is true, why is it at the very end? If it is so important, shouldn't it be at the very beginning? You usually first deal with the important stuff, then the rest falls into place. But in the catechism, it appears that prayer is being dealt with as if it were some afterthought. Perhaps that is true throughout our lives as well.

Isn't that how prayer often incorrectly functions in our own lives? "If all else fails," we may think, "then you can still pray. That may be the only thing you can do at that point. But at least there is still that one thing left."

Is that also the reasoning of the catechism?

Well, prayer is dealt with already at the beginning of the Heidelberg Catechism, for in Lord's Day three, we are told about the creation of man and what it was like before his fall into sin. It says, "God created man . . . so that he might rightly know God his Creator, heartily love Him, and live with Him in eternal blessedness to praise and glorify Him."

That is what prayer is all about. God created us to praise and glorify him and to live with him in eternal blessedness. There were no obstacles in the way between God and humans. There was total harmony.

For what is prayer? Prayer is the expression of our life with God without any hindrances, without any obstacles. It is praising and glorifying him for the wonderful relationship that he has established with us. That is the way it was in Paradise before the fall into sin.

Sin, however, put an end to that. Communication between God and his people became completely broken. Only God himself can restore the lines of communication. That is what the middle section of the Heidelberg Catechism dealt with extensively. There, we are told about how our Lord and Saviour, Jesus Christ, restored the lines of communication through his death and resurrection.

And so, it is no wonder that prayer is dealt with at the very end. In his final act, the Lord Jesus, having risen from the dead, ascended into heaven and seated himself at the right hand of God the Father, opening the gates of heaven.

And now, this very last section of the catechism reminds us

that the lines of communication have been restored and tells us what that means, namely that we must also make use of those open lines of communication. And it teaches us how.

Vibrant communication channels are crucial, no matter where we live here on earth. Without effective means of communication, people and whole countries are isolated. Lack of communication causes turmoil, distrust, chaos, loneliness, and helplessness.

Think about what happens when, because of war or natural disasters, an entire area or a whole country is devastated. The most important thing that needs to be done after such devastations is restoring the lines of communication. The power lines and phone and other communication lines must be repaired. The radio and TV stations and internet providers must be able to send out their signals again. Phone lines and hydroelectric lines must also be repaired. Only once these things have been done can you return to normal, to how it used to be.

That is the way it is with our prayer. But prayer is much more critical. Prayer refers to the lines of communication between God and us. And a connection with God is essential for your spiritual and eternal well-being. Prayer indicates that lines of communication between God and us are restored. Prayer is vital for the life of a Christian. Indeed, you cannot call yourself a Christian if you don't know how to pray. The nature of prayer is the subject of this last chapter of my book.

Scripture

Exodus 30:1–10

The Altar of Incense

30 "You shall make an altar on which to burn incense; you shall make it of acacia wood.

2 A cubit shall be its length, and a cubit its breadth. It shall be square, and two cubits shall be its height. Its horns shall be of one piece with it.

3 You shall overlay it with pure gold, its top and around its sides and its horns. And you shall make a molding of gold around it.

4 And you shall make two golden rings for it. Under its molding on two opposite sides of it you shall make them, and they shall be holders for poles with which to carry it.

5 You shall make the poles of acacia wood and overlay them with gold.

6 And you shall put it in front of the veil that is above the ark of the testimony, in front of the mercy seat that is above the testimony, where I will meet with you.

7 And Aaron shall burn fragrant incense on it. Every morning when he dresses the lamps he shall burn it,

8 and when Aaron sets up the lamps at twilight, he shall burn it, a regular incense offering before the Lord throughout your generations.

9 You shall not offer unauthorized incense on it, or a burnt offering, or a grain offering, and you shall not pour a drink offering on it.

10 Aaron shall make atonement on its horns once a year. With the blood of the sin offering of atonement he shall make atonement for it once in the year throughout your generations. It is most holy to the Lord."

James 1:1-8

Greeting
1 James, a servant of God and of the Lord Jesus Christ, To the twelve tribes in the Dispersion: Greetings.

Testing of Your Faith
2 Count it all joy, my brothers, when you meet trials of various kinds,

3 for you know that the testing of your faith produces steadfastness.

4 And let steadfastness have its full effect, that you may be perfect and complete, lacking in nothing.

5 If any of you lacks wisdom, let him ask God, who gives generously to all without reproach, and it will be given him.

6 But let him ask in faith, with no doubting, for the one who doubts is like a wave of the sea that is driven and tossed by the wind.

7 For that person must not suppose that he will receive anything from the Lord;

8 he is a double-minded man, unstable in all his ways.

Heidelberg Catechism

Lord's Day 45

116. Q. Why is prayer necessary for Christians?

A. Because prayer is the most important part
of the thankfulness
which God requires of us.[1]

Moreover, God will give
his grace and the Holy Spirit
only to those who constantly
and with heartfelt longing
ask him for these gifts
and thank him for them.[2]

[1] Ps 50:14, 15; 116:12–19; 1 Thess 5:16–18.
[2] Mt 7:7, 8; Lk 11:9–13.

117. Q. What belongs to a prayer
      which pleases God
      and is heard by him?

   A. First,
      we must from the heart
      call upon the one true God only,
      who has revealed himself in his Word,
      for all that he has commanded us to pray.[1]

      Second,
      we must thoroughly know
      our need and misery,
      so that we may humble ourselves
      before God.[2]

      Third,
      we must rest on this firm foundation
      that, although we do not deserve it,
      God will certainly hear our prayer
      for the sake of Christ our Lord,
      as he has promised us in his Word.[3]

[1] Ps 145:18–20; Jn 4:22–24; Rom 8:26, 27; Jas 1:5; 1 Jn 5:14, 15; Rev 19:10.
[2] 2 Chron 7:14; 20:12; Ps 2:11; 34:18; 62:8; Is 66:2; Rev 4.
[3] Dan 9:17–19; Mt 7:8; Jn 14:13, 14; 16:23; Rom 10:13; Jas 1:6.

118. Q. What has God commanded us
      to ask of him?

   A. All the things we need
      for body and soul,[1]
      as included in the Lord's prayer
      which Christ our Lord himself taught us.

[1] Mt 6:33; Jas 1:17.

Peace through Prayer

At War with the Enemy

When Adam and Eve, at the instigation of the devil, rebelled against God in Paradise, there was war. This is explicitly stated in Genesis 3, where God attributes the beginning of enmity between the offspring of the woman and the offspring of the serpent to Adam and Eve's sinful disobedience. It signified a state of war.

Warring parties do not communicate with each other. Instead, they strive to annihilate each other. Satan's aim was to destroy God, an endeavour that proved unsuccessful. Consequently, he resorted to the next wicked course of action. He tried to destroy everything that belongs to God, including God's children. That is still his game. And he uses every trick in the book and tries to cut off every means of communication between God and us by whatever means.

That's also what we see when there's a war between nations. Then, the warring parties will do everything in their power to bring down the lines of communication. They will bomb the radio and TV stations so that no information can go out to the people.

Those at war will keep any people they capture from communicating with their own side. They want them to be totally cut off from any contact with their nation, homes, and families. In place of communication, they will only feed limited and false information that will demoralize them, for they do not want to give them any hope. In this way, they ensure that no help will come to them.

That is the way it is, for example, with the country of North Korea right now. It is at war with the rest of the world. For that reason, the leaders there have shut down the lines of communication with the Western world and even with China, their closest ally. Their own people are not allowed to have any contact with the rest of the world.

That is what Satan does. He does not want you to be in communication with God, and he will do everything in his power to keep you from fellowship with God. Satan is out to destroy you. He is out to demoralize you. He is constantly feeding you false information, putting false fear into the hearts of the people, making them think that they are stronger than they are and that the enemy is weak. He wants to take away hope.

For that reason, it is so important for us to be in constant communion with God. Without communion with God, you will be destroyed. You need to pray. But in order to pray, you have to be properly informed about God's desire for intimate dialogue with him. You have to understand that prayer is the expression of your covenant relationship with God.

Satan Already Lost the War

And so, what does God want you to know? The most important thing he wants you to know is that Satan has already lost the war. Oh sure, there are still many little battles happening here and there. But the war has been won. Jesus Christ is the victor, and so are all those who belong to him. And you need to be reminded of that time and again.

God's people in the Old Testament also had to know about that impending victory. For that reason, God promised a Redeemer. He made that promise already in Paradise. He promised that the offspring of the woman would crush the serpent, Satan (Genesis 3:15).

He made that promise because the Lord God does not want

us to be at war. Therefore, he also wants to restore the lines of communication, which he did through his Son Jesus Christ. While he was still on earth, the Lord Jesus said that he is the door through whom his sheep may enter the sheepfold. No one can come to the Father except through him (John 6:44). When Christ ascended into heaven and sat down at the right hand of God, he made that access for his children a certainty, for he laid down his life for the sheep so that that could come about.

Who exactly are those sheep? Well, take careful note of the way question 116 in Lord's Day 45 of the Heidelberg Catechism is phrased. It asks, "Why is prayer necessary for *Christians*?" It uses the word *Christians*. In Q&A 32 of the catechism, we are asked why we are called Christians. It says there that we are called Christians because we are members of Christ by faith. We belong to him because of our faith.

Such faith, however, must be an active faith. Those who have faith do not just sit back and do nothing. No, they act in accordance with that faith. It is not so that Christ has done it all and that now his children are left passive. No, on the contrary, Christ also showed his children how to keep the lines of communication with God open. That is through prayer. Prayer is a very necessary and integral part of our relationship with God.

For that reason, the Lord Jesus also gave the Lord's Prayer to his disciples and to all of us. He gave them that prayer because he *wanted* them to pray. It is a command.

However, there is a problem. Because of sin, we have lost the ability to speak to God. And so we must be taught how to pray.

There is a lot of praying that goes on in this world. People pray for this and that and for everything else. Much of it, however, is worthless. In chapter 4:3 of his letter, James says, "You ask and do not receive, because you ask wrongly." That is a problem for us as well. We do not always pray for the right things or in the right manner.

Exodus 30 describes the altar of incense. The burning of incense symbolized the prayers going up to God. That altar was overlaid with gold and placed before God by the curtain of the holy of holies, the most holy sanctuary. Why did that particular altar have to be made of gold? Why not made of bronze or some other kind of metal? Well, because of the great value of prayer. Our prayers are precious to him.

Does that sound strange to your ears? For he is the Almighty God, the Creator of heaven and earth, but we are just mere creatures. Why does he value our input and thoughts that we send up to him? When God created humans, he said that they shall "have dominion over the fish of the sea and over the birds of the heavens and over the livestock and over all the earth and over every creeping thing that creeps on the earth" (Genesis 1:26).

Although he is the Almighty God, it pleases him to work through those of us on earth. Such a rule involves not just people's labour and sweat but also their thoughts and involvement. It must take place not just among people but also with God. You see, that is what prayer is about. God wants our prayers. They are of immense value to him.

Prayer must be based on an intimate knowledge of who God is in relationship to us. There are those who have difficulty with prayer. They do not know what to say. And so they pray the same kinds of prayers time and again. They offer up empty, well-worn phrases. It is not an intimate dialogue with God.

The Essence of Prayer

But what is prayer? Prayer is the expression of your covenant relationship. And if you know what it means to live within that covenant relationship, then you will also know how to pray. Then you will not be at a loss for words. You will know what to say and what to pray for.

The catechism says that prayer is necessary because God will only give to those who ask. You may wonder, is that true? Doesn't God already know what I need? That's also what it says in Psalm 139:4: "Even before a word is on my tongue, behold, O LORD, you know it altogether." Why, then, should we ask?

Well, God gives us the example of the prayers of the patriarchs. Think about how Abraham pleaded with God about Sodom and Gomorrah. God listened to him and postponed his judgement (Genesis 18:22–33). What about Moses and how he prayed to God about the Israelites that God would not wipe them off the face of the earth because of their sins? God heard him (Exodus 32:7–14).

Does that mean that God changes his mind because we talk to him? Did God, for example, change his mind because of Moses's plea and consequently not destroy the Israelites? Moses and all those patriarchs whose prayers were heard knew the mind of God. Moses knew that God wanted a people to serve him, so God worked Moses's plea into his plan. But it is clear that God was pleased to listen to sinners like them and us to accomplish his plan.

If you want your prayers to be heard, you must know how God deals with his people. Then, you can also make requests from God. But only requests that are based on the promises that he makes. You can demand from God to feed you physically and spiritually, for example. Because that's what he promised he would do. You can ask him to forgive you your sins. Because that's also what he promised he would do. Of course, you must do it from the heart. You have to do it knowing you are undeserving because of your sin. And that also has to be expressed. Nevertheless, God wants you to ask these things from him. He wants you to be in communion with him—all the time.

You must understand God's plan for you and for this world. He is bringing this world to a glorious end. And you and me with it. When you pray to him with that knowledge and with that in mind, then he will also grant your requests.

Of course, we can't understand the interplay between God's sovereign plan and our involvement in prayer in bringing God's plan into effect. We are too little and too weak for that. It is hard for us to understand everything that happens. But it is enough to know that although he is sovereign, he nevertheless uses our prayers. Because if you believe in him, you can be sure that you are a child of his. And he loves to hear from you and me. He *must* hear from you and me.

Prayer is an expression of faith. If you genuinely believe that God exists, that he created all things, and that he provides every single thing in your life, then you cannot help but speak to him about it and thank him for these gifts. Then, when you see the sun rise, and when you see the grass grow, and the animals being looked after in the field and in the forests and in the air, and when you receive food on your table, you cannot help but speak to your heavily Father about that, for he supplies his creatures with all those things. Then, you'll want to pour out your heart to him and give thanks to him.

Someone who has studied God's Word fully realizes that whatever they receive, they receive out of grace alone. Because of sin, we deserve eternal damnation. And it is only through God's grace that we receive so many beautiful things.

Someone who truly knows the Lord also knows deep in their heart that whatever they receive, they receive for their own good. For there are times when God does withhold certain things from us. We ask him for them, but we do not receive them. We think that we really need to receive what we are asking for. And we could not imagine why God would withhold it.

And yet, sometimes he does. For example, you may ardently pray for a promotion at work but instead you are inexplicably let go. It is painful and confusing when that happens. But then another opportunity opens up which is much better and more suitable. And then we thank God for such an outcome. Things do not always go according to our plans. And that is why we have to trust in God, for if you know the ways of the Lord, then you submit yourself to his will. And you are at peace no matter what happens.

Do you think your heavenly Father, who gave his own Son to shed his blood for you, would wish any harm upon you? As the Lord Jesus says in the Sermon on the Mount, in Matthew 7, what earthly father would give his own son a serpent instead of a fish or a stone instead of a piece of bread?

If that sense of generous love is how it is with your earthly father, imagine what it is with your heavenly Father. The Lord God will never give you anything to harm you. Whatever he sends your way, he sends for your good. It may seem like an evil thing to us sometimes, but it isn't. God will use whatever comes to us in this life for our good. And when we pray to the Lord our God, we acknowledge him as a faithful and loving Father. As we read in the letter of James, God gives generously to all people.

But we must ask in faith. We must not doubt, for those who doubt are like a wave of the sea that is driven and tossed by the wind. No, the Lord your God is concerned about you. He is concerned about your eternal well-being.

As I said, prayer is only for believers. It is for those who know the will of the Lord and want to do the will of the Lord. If you know God, you also know that you are to fight against your sins with all your might. Those who lie and cheat habitually without remorse and who then lift up their hands in prayer to God will not, as it says in Isaiah 1:15, be able to see God's face, for it will be hidden from them. And those who refuse to forgive others their sins cannot expect God to forgive them their own sins either, even though they pray for it. And it does not make sense either to ask for riches from God, who tells us in Matthew 19:24 that it is easier for a camel to go through the eye of a needle than for a rich man to enter the kingdom of God.

Even children know that there are certain things that parents will not give them. "No use asking him," they say of their father, "because he will not give it to us anyway." In the same way, we ought to know our heavenly Father. We ought to know what we can and cannot ask for. We ought to understand what a legitimate request is and what is not. As Paul says in Ephesians 5:17, "Do not be foolish, but understand what the Lord's will is."

The Lord Jesus said in the sermon on the Mount, "Your Father knows what you need before you ask him" (Matthew 6:8). That does not mean that you do not have to tell him, but it means that you cannot lead him astray.

At one time, some people brought to Jesus a paralytic, a person who could not get up for his most natural needs and wants. You would think that when he was lying there, at the feet of the Lord Jesus, his real needs were evident to everyone. That man needed to be healed! But what did the Lord Jesus say? He said, "Son, your sins are forgiven." Christ identified and provided for the man's deepest need.

We must know what is good for us. That is why in answer 116 of the Heidelberg Catechism, the two most essential items that we need are identified: God's grace and his Holy Spirit. There is nothing more important than those two.

Why do we need God's grace so desperately? We need it because of our fall into sin. We need it because also within our hearts and minds, there are always wars going on. Satan wants you to think that you can do without God, that whatever this world has to offer you is all you need. He tells you that you can be your own saviour. He gives you false information and false hope all the time. And how often do we not fall for his dirty tricks?

Without God's grace, we would perish internally. For God's grace refers to his mercy. It refers to his compassion like a mother has for her baby. A good mother has great compassion for the child in her womb. A real mother would not want any harm to come to her baby. Well, that is also how it is with God and his children. But we need to pray for God's grace. The Lord wants us to realize that we need him and cannot live without him.

And we need his Holy Spirit. For the Holy Spirit brings to mind what God has taught us. The Holy Spirit softens our hearts so that we want the lines of communication to be open between God and us. The Holy Spirit makes everything well between God and us. Through the Holy Spirit, there is no more war between God and us. God has drawn us over to his side, to the victorious side. And therefore, when we pray to him, he will listen to us. You and he are on the same side. Remember that when you pray, and the peace of God will come upon you.

Reflection

1. In Philippians 4:6, we are comforted against anxiety. We are told that, by prayer and supplication, with thanksgiving, we may let our requests be made known to God. Are you willing to pour out your heart and express your thankfulness to him for saving you from the grip of Satan?

2. How do you experience hope in knowing that Jesus Christ desires your intimate dialogue with him? How do you find joy in knowing that prayer is the expression of your covenant relationship with God?

Acknowledgements

This book of sermons would not have come to fruition without the invaluable assistance and encouragement of many cherished individuals. In my introduction, I mention how my son David and his colleague Norbert Elliot planted the initial seeds for this book. Their contributions went far beyond that. Along with Norbert's wife, Frances, who provided steadfast support in the background, they were instrumental from start to finish.

I am deeply grateful to my esteemed colleagues, Arjan de Visser, Jack Visscher, and Richard Aasman, for their insightful contributions and meticulous proofreading. My heartfelt thanks go to my wife, Barbara, whose critical and loving support has been invaluable throughout my ministry. Above all, I thank the Lord God, whose grace and guidance, despite my many weaknesses and shortcomings, have allowed me to be a herald of good tidings for these many years.

About the Author

WILLEM B. SLOMP, BA, BSW, M.Div. is Pastor Emeritus of the Immanuel Canadian Reformed Church in Edmonton. He previously served churches in Houston, British Columbia and Neerlandia, Alberta. He and his wife, Barbara, have been blessed with seven children, twenty-four grandchildren, and three great-grandchildren. Willem lives in Edmonton, Alberta.

www.ingramcontent.com/pod-product-compliance
Lightning Source LLC
Chambersburg PA
CBHW060317050426
42449CB00011B/2515